COMMUNICATION STRATEGIES

Applied Language Studies
Edited by David Crystal and Keith Johnson

This new series aims to deal with key topics within the main branches of applied language studies − initially in the fields of foreign language teaching and learning, child language acquisition and clinical or remedial language studies. The series will provide students with a research perspective in a particular topic, at the same time containing an original slant which will make each volume a genuine contribution to the development of ideas in the subject.

Series List

Communication Strategies
A Psychological Analysis of Second-Language Use
Ellen Bialystok

Chomsky's Universal Grammar
An Introduction
V. J. Cook

Principles of Language Testing
Alan Davies

Instructed Second Language Acquisition
Learning in the Classroom
Rod Ellis

The ELT Curriculum
Design, Innovation and Management
Ronald V. White

COMMUNICATION STRATEGIES

A Psychological Analysis of Second-Language Use

Ellen Bialystok

Basil Blackwell

First published 1990

Basil Blackwell Ltd
108 Cowley Road, Oxford, OX4 1JF, UK

Basil Blackwell, Inc.
3 Cambridge Center
Cambridge, Massachusetts 02142, USA

British Library Cataloguing in Publication Data

A CIP catalogue record for this book is available from the
British Library.

Library of Congress Cataloging in Publication Data

Bialystok, Ellen.
    Communication strategies/Ellen Bialystok.
        p. cm. — (Applied language studies)
    Includes bibliographical references.
    ISBN 0−631−17457−5 — ISBN 0−631−17458−3 (pbk)
    1. Second-language acquisition.   2. Oral communication.
I. Title.   II. Series.
P118.2.B5 1990
401′.93 − dc20   89−48322
                                                          CIP

Typeset in 10 on 12 pt Ehrhardt
by Setrite
Printed in Great Britain by T.J. Press Ltd, Padstow, Cornwall

Contents

Preface   vi

1   Defining Strategies   1

2   Identifying Communication Strategies   14

3   Taxonomies of Communication Strategies   37

4   Empirical Evaluation of the Taxonomies   57

5   Communicating in a First Language   84

6   Investigations of Second-Language Use   104

7   Language Acquisition and Language Processing   116

8   Learning and Teaching Communication Strategies   139

Notes   148

References   150

Index   159

Preface

This book is an examination of a very simple problem: how do you manage to communicate when you have limited command of a language? The problem is most apparent for adults trying to speak in a second language which they have not perfectly mastered. It is most apparent in those cases because first, adults tend to make a great fuss about such limitations, and second, because the disparity between what the adult might have said in a native language and what they manage to say in a second language is so striking.

Systematic study of this problem for (usually adult) second-language learners has been ongoing for about fifteen years and comprises the sub-area of second-language acquisition research that has become known as *communication strategies*. Considerable theory and research has accumulated in this sub-area and interesting modelling has been developed.

The main point I shall argue is that parcelling out this sub-area as a distinct domain of inquiry concerned with a unique phenomenon is counterproductive. The utterances of second-language learners that are deposited in the lists of examples of communication strategies need to be explained, but my claim is that they do not need an explanation that is any different from the one we need to explain a variety of other phenomena of language use. What we need instead is a sufficiently powerful model of language processing that will include as part of its functioning the specific irregularities of speech that become designated as communication strategies. Communication strategies, that is, are not aberrations, but part of normal language use.

The book is organized around the examination of three issues relevant to an investigation of communication strategies. The first issue is that of *identification*: what is the domain of behaviour that is included in the topic? This is covered in chapters 2, 3, and 4. The second is that of *explanation*: what processes of language use can accommodate these behaviours? These issues are explored in chapters 5, 6, and 7. The third is that of *instruction*: what consequences for language instruction follow from this conception? Pedagogical implications are discussed in chapter 8. A model for using this three-issue approach to investigate strategies is outlined in chapter 1 in a review of the literature on children's problem-solving strategies. There are two reasons for including that discussion. First, the literature on children's problem-solving strategies clarifies the integral role of the three issues of identification, explanation, and instruction for an apparently different domain. Second, a closer examination of the problems and solutions evident in that literature shows that the strategies responsible for second-language communication and children's problem-solving may not be so different. In that case, it would be profitable to study solutions proposed for one as a means of understanding the other.

The primary focus of the book is on the explanation of communication strategies, but that explanation must follow from a clear definition of what constitutes a communication strategy for a second-language learner. The two main approaches in the second-language literature to identifying communication strategies are the use of theoretical definition and descriptive taxonomy. These are reviewed in chapters 2 and 3 respectively. The fourth chapter pursues the taxonomic approach in detail by presenting empirical evidence from a study of children's use of communication strategies in a second language.

By the end of chapter 4, there is a certain frustration apparent in the discussion. Most of the systems considered for defining, identifying, and classifying communication strategies examined in the first four chapters were ultimately considered inadequate. Yet the intention is by no means to be negative. Rather, the work that is reviewed in the first four chapters forms the essential basis of the next step. The conclusion is that what is missing from the work covered in the traditional descriptive approaches is a mechanism for processing that will explain *how* learners produce these utterances, and *why* they choose the solutions they do. What is missing, in other words, is a treatment of the second issue, namely, an explanation for strategic communication.

The discussion of this second issue begins by examining the explanations developed for related problems in language use. An obvious place to begin is children learning their first language. Like the adult second-language learner, children would like to say more than their linguistic resources allow. How children cope with this problem and the implications of their solutions for our inquiry are considered in chapter 5. The next chapter reviews some attempts to take a more process-oriented approach to the description of oral language utterances. This approach provides an important bridge between theory and description: we want to find a theoretical explanation without losing sight of the actual utterances that speakers produce. Chapter 7 outlines a theoretical model of language processing that has the capacity to incorporate communication strategies into its operation.

This book was written while I was a visiting scholar in the Department of Experimental Psychology at the University of Oxford. I am indebted to Peter Bryant and to the special group of visitors who provided a remarkable atmosphere of friendship and scholarship.

I acknowledge with appreciation the financial support for research and writing that I received in the form of a research grant from the Natural Sciences and Engineering Research Council of Canada and an exchange fellowship from the Royal Society of Britain.

The manuscript also profited from friends and colleagues who read earlier versions and provided suggestions and comments, or debated theory with me. I am thus indebted to Ruth Berman, Shoshana Blum-Kulka, Judith Codd, Annette Karmiloff-Smith, Paul Meara, Chris Pratt, Mike Sharwood Smith, and Bernard Spolsky. Eric Kellerman provided comments through every known medium of communication − letter, telephone, conversation, written comment on draft, and e-mail.

The most important ingredient in producing this work is my family − Frank, Sandra, and Lauren − who allowed me to tear them away from home so that I could indulge in a fantasy for a year.

1 Defining Strategies

While living in Colombia, a friend of mine wanted to buy some silk. The Spanish word for silk, *seda*, however, is apparently also used for a variety of synthetic substitutes. Eager to have the genuine product, my friend went into the local shop and, roughly translated from Spanish, said something like the following to the shopkeeper: 'It's made by little animals, for their house, and then turned into material.' In addition to lacking an unambiguous word for silk, she found herself unable to find the Spanish words for *silkworm* or *cocoon*.

Convoluted descriptions such as these are a routine part of speech when one is trying to communicate in a second language. The familiar ease and fluency with which we sail from one idea to the next in our first language is constantly shattered by some gap in our knowledge of a second language. The gap can take many forms − a word, a structure, a phrase, a tense marker, an idiom. Our attempts to overcome these gaps have been called *communication strategies*.

What is deceptive about the label 'communication strategy' is that it vaguely refers to a notion that makes intuitive sense to both researchers in applied linguistics and nonprofessional language learners. The concept superficially refers to some identifiable part of language behaviour that most people would feel confident that they could identify. If there is less certainty about why strategies occur or how they work, these same people would probably feel certain that a little more study by appropriate specialists would answer these questions.

But the popular belief that it is a straightforward matter to determine what constitutes a strategy belies the fact that vigorous debate among researchers has failed to yield a universally acceptable definition. The everyday use of the term in sport ('the team adopted a defensive strategy'), military ('the general's strategy was to cut off the enemy's retreat'), and management ('the management's strategy was to cut costs by reducing the workforce') contexts exacerbates the problem by equating the term with wilful planning to achieve explicit goals. Yet this everyday meaning does not necessarily extend to the special uses required when 'strategy' is used as a technical term for an aspect of communication.

In order to arrive at an explicit technical definition for communication strategy, it is necessary to see how the concept fits into a larger framework in which the notion of strategy is invoked as part of language acquisition and language use. The broader view from language processing may ultimately require that descriptions of strategies are integrated into even larger explanations for cognition, language use being part of cognition. Piecemeal approaches which disregard systems developed in response to related problems in other areas of cognitive and linguistic processing will ultimately prove limited. The position adopted in this volume is that an explanation of communication strategies for second-language learners must build on existing frameworks developed to address related problems in other areas. These related areas include first-language acquisition and communication and, perhaps more marginally, cognitive problem-solving.

The approach is thus an integrative one: first, second-language communication strategies are placed within the broader context of communication strategies for a first or second language; second, these communication strategies are considered for their relation to even more general cognitive strategies. The purpose is to find the most general level of explanation that adequately accounts for all these phenomena. It would seem odd if the cognitive mechanisms that produced communication strategies in a second language were fundamentally different from those responsible for the strategic use of a first language. Similarly, both these processes should bear important similarities to the mental processes involved in strategic cognition in a variety of domains.

Equally important as the search for a set of common processes is the identification and preservation of the uniqueness of second-language communication strategies. At some level of generality, explanations cease to explain anything at all. The special features and distinctive constraints that characterize communication in a second language need to be given serious attention and require explicit treatment in these explanations. The two guiding principles, therefore, are a search for the most general level of explanation that offers a model of the process of using communication strategies and a description and explanation of what makes those processes unique when communication is taking place in a second language.

This chapter will begin with a survey of the way in which communication strategies have been defined for second-language learners. Three features of strategies indicated by these definitions will be identified and evaluated. This evaluation will set out some of the major themes that will be pursued throughout the book.

The second section of the chapter will present a brief survey of the way in which cognitive strategy has been used as an explanation for children's problem-solving. Like adults attempting to speak in a weak language, children are often restricted in their solutions to problems by an incomplete repertoire of skills or an inadequate basis of knowledge. Also like adults, they confront these challenges by adopting certain strategies. The theoretical problems of identifying, conceptualizing, and explaining these strategies anticipate the corresponding problems encountered by applied linguistics in explaining communication strategies. Accordingly, the lessons of the endeavour to explain children's strategies will be explicated so that they can guide the efforts to explain the communication strategies of second-language learners.

Definitions of Communication Strategies

Consider the following definitions which have been proposed for the communication strategies of second-language learners:

> a systematic technique employed by a speaker to express his meaning when faced with some difficulty;
>
> (Corder, 1977)

> a mutual attempt of two interlocutors to agree on a meaning in situations where requisite meaning structures are not shared;
>
> (Tarone, 1980)

> potentially conscious plans for solving what to an individual presents itself as a problem in reaching a particular communicative goal;
>
> (Faerch and Kasper, 1983a)

> techniques of coping with difficulties in communicating in an imperfectly known second language.
>
> (Stern, 1983)

Although different in detail, the definitions converge on three features: *problematicity, consciousness*, and *intentionality*. Each of these features will be examined and discussed for their role in a definition of communication strategies.

Characteristics Identified in Definitions

Problematicity Perhaps the most basic and prevalent feature cited in the definitions of communication strategies is problematicity. It is the idea that strategies are used only when a speaker perceives that there is a problem which may interrupt communication. This restriction of strategies to instances of difficulty corresponds to our common-sense use of the term. But is problematicity also characteristic of communication strategies?

There are two implications of proposing problematicity as a defining feature of communication strategies. First, the way in which speakers use language strategically, that is, when strategies are being employed, would need to be kept distinct from the way in which those speakers used language nonstrategically, that is, for ordinary communication. Although several models that will be discussed in this volume explicitly acknowledge that distinction, it is not clear how the distinction would be realized in actual language processing.

What, in fact, is different about the way in which language is used in these two circumstances? Such issues would need to be addressed if problematicity is used to signify the use of strategies.

A second implication of using problematicity as a defining feature is that it leaves uncertain the status of communicative language use that is not normally perceived as problematic but which none the less may be strategic. Native speakers, for example, frequently provide lengthy definitions for words to ensure that the listener has understood even though no communicative problem has been encountered. Some speech acts, such as explanations, invariably include the types of descriptions that would have been classified as communication strategies had they been spoken by a second-language learner: 'You take this street to the place where there is a round park in the centre and many roads come together.' This utterance could have been spoken by a non-native speaker of English who did not know the word *roundabout* or by a native speaker of English addressing a North American visitor who had not yet had the dizzying experience of driving on one (and therefore did not know what it was). Using problematicity as criterial, the utterance would be a strategy in one case but not the other. Hence, it is not clear that problematicity accurately delineates the domain of second-language communication strategies.

It is undeniable that there is a significant portion of communication in a second language that is clearly problematic. In these cases, speakers and listeners alike would have no hesitation in recognizing those instances and identifying the strategies that were used. To claim that problematicity is not criterial to a definition is to assert that this feature is not *defining* of communication strategies. Communication strategies can occur in the absence of problematicity.

Consciousness   Consciousness is implicit in most of the definitions proposed for communication strategies. If communication strategies are truly conscious events of language use, then it follows that speakers who employ them are aware (to some extent, in some undefined way) of having done so. Yet it is not self-evident that speakers are indeed aware that their utterances constitute strategic uses of language. Communication always involves choice, and the choices evident when a strategy has been used may have been made no more or less consciously than any other choice. Speakers routinely choose among multiple labels for objects: *dog* or *collie* referring to a choice among category levels, *truck* or *lorry* referring to a choice among dialects, and so on. In communicative contexts, these choices serve strategic purposes and perhaps avoid potential misunderstanding by the listener. The choices, however, may be made entirely without the conscious consideration of the speaker.

Using consciousness as a criterion also has the rather restricting implication that strategy use is available only to those speakers for whom conscious reflection is possible. The major group excluded by this feature is children, for whom it is usually claimed that conscious monitoring of their cognitive processing is not possible. This issue will be discussed in the second section of this chapter. Yet much of the language used by children appears to make use of the same strategies as does the speech of adult second-language learners. Some examples of children's strategic use of language will be discussed in chapters 5 and 6.

Although Faerch and Kasper (1983a) include consciousness as a feature of communication strategies, they recognize an indeterminacy about it. They acknowledge that the plans that speakers develop as part of the process of language production may or may not be conscious and that this consciousness may change on different occasions. Hence they conclude that strategies are *potentially* conscious plans. But without some independent means of deciding which plans could potentially be conscious, one is left to assume that *all* plans are potentially conscious. Hence there is no means of distinguishing plans that lead to strategic speech from those that do not by virtue of consciousness.

Intentionality Intentionality refers to the learner's control over a repertoire of strategies so that particular ones may be selected from the range of options and deliberately applied to achieve certain effects. This aspect of the definitions is conveyed by the assumption that the speaker has control over the strategy that is selected and that the choice is responsive to the perceived problem. Such intentionality presupposes consciousness, but even setting aside the possible complications of considering the consciousness of the strategies, applying the criterion of intentionality itself leads to some dilemmas.

The implication of communication strategies being intentional is that there would be systematic relations between the use of specific communication strategies and specific conditions of the communicative situation. Thus, one would expect that learners would select a strategy according to some relevant factor, such as the learner's level of proficiency with the language, the nature of the concept being communicated, the conditions under which communication is occurring, and so on. Yet the research exploring such links has revealed little basis for making claims about the systematic selection of strategies. These studies are reviewed in chapter 3. Accordingly, the intentionality of communication strategies is questionable.

The ambiguities attributed to each of the three identifying criteria that are implicated in the definitions casts an imprecision upon these definitions. But is the failure to isolate clear predictive characteristics a problem with the definitions or a problem with the concept of strategies? The argument that will be advanced in this book is that the concept of second-language communication strategy, as traditionally used in the field, cannot be defined exclusively by reference to its unique features. As will be argued in chapter 7, communication strategies are continuous with 'ordinary' language processing and cannot be severed from it by virtue of distinctive features.

Towards an Explanation of Communication Strategies

Researchers investigating the way in which adults learn and use a second language recognized some time ago that there is an important part of that process which appears to be unique to second-language activities and that sets it apart from prior experiences in learning and using a first language. Early references to the strategies of learning and using a second language are evidence of the conviction by these researchers that these strategies would ultimately have a central role in explanations of second-language acquisition (e.g. Selinker, 1972; Stern, 1975). In the past decade, more focused attempts at identifying, defining, and explaining these strategies have been undertaken. The general direction of those attempts is conveyed by the definitions listed at the beginning of this chapter. Research in communication strategies, that is, has essentially been motivated by these definitions.

A closer examination of the definitions, however, shows that the characteristics that are identified as being indicative of communication strategies are each obscured by some question. It may be that a radically different approach will be necessary to identify with any certainty and to explain with any conviction how these strategies function for second-language learners. Again, the attempt at explaining second-language communication strategies that will be pursued here will be to import processing models from other related domains and adapt them to the special characteristics of communication strategies.

Three issues need to be addressed in constructing a description of strategy use by learners in any domain. The first is to determine a rationally consistent means for *identifying* strategic behaviour and distinguishing it from what might be considered nonstrategic behaviour within that domain. The second is to *explain* this behaviour through an analysis of that portion of speech that is deemed strategic. This would include addressing such problems as how learners select and apply strategies in specific problem situations and how those strategic solutions differ from nonstrategic ones. The third is to assess the prognosis for *instruction* in the strategies considered to be effective so that learners can improve in their ability to solve certain problems.

This book is organized around the examination of the three issues of identifying, explaining, and teaching strategies. Two major approaches have been used in the literature on communication strategies to address the first issue of identifying the strategies. These are the definitional and taxonomic approaches, and they are discussed in chapters 2 and 3 respectively. An evaluation of the taxonomic descriptions as an explanation (second issue) for these strategies is presented in chapter 4. In response to some of the weaknesses of the taxonomic approach identified in that evaluation, two other areas of literature are reviewed for their possible relevance to an explanation. These are strategies used in first-language communication, especially by children (chapter 5) and strategies used by second-language learners in special situations (chapter 6). On the basis of findings from these areas, a framework for explaining how communication strategies might function in language processing is offered in chapter 7. Finally, the third issue, pedagogy, is addressed in the last chapter.

To illustrate how these three issues contribute to an explanation of strategic behaviour and to anticipate the problems that will be encountered in the analysis of communication strategies, the following section will describe strategic behaviour in another domain – children's use of strategies to solve cognitive problems. This domain provides a parallel case of a group of inexperienced subjects attempting to perform in situations that exceed their ability.

Children's Problem-Solving Strategies

The research on the strategic behaviour shown by children when solving problems is an interesting place to grapple with the three issues that constitute an explanation of strategy use. Much of this research is concerned with children's approaches to school-related problems, such as reading (Brown, 1980; Forrest-Pressley and Gillies, 1983), solving mathematics problems (Siegler, 1987a), and remembering (Flavell and Wellman, 1977) so the influence of instruction on performance is central. The research goals are to identify the range of possible solutions to specific problems, to account for the choices children make at different times in their mastery of these problems, and to determine the relation between specific choices and success.

Identifying Cognitive Strategies

The first issue is identification: on what basis can strategic solutions be distinguished from nonstrategic ones? Consider the following examples.

An infant, 18 months old, reaches across a high-chair table to pull a string that is attached to a desired toy. Alas, the string is too far away. In a moment of inspiration, the child realizes that a long hook-like stick, fortuitously left on the table by some generous (or nefariously empirical) researcher can be used to retrieve the toy and solve the problem. Another infant in the same high-chair several minutes later, fails to notice the potential of the stick and pulls desperately on the high-chair table until the string can be reached. According to Brown (1987), the first solution is an example of strategic behaviour while the second, a vain attempt to solve the problem through brute force, is not.

A 7-year-old child is sitting in an arithmetic class, tormented by the possibility that she may be called upon to solve an addition problem. Inevitably, her turn arrives. How to calculate the required sum? A quick surreptitious check of her concealed fingers delivers the correct solution. Next, her friend is asked a similar problem. Quickly, the solution is recited from a memorized set. Siegler (1987a) claims that the finger counting used by the first child is an example of strategic behaviour; the retrieval used by the second child may be more desirable, more efficient, and more correct, but it is not strategic.

What constitutes strategic behaviour? In the broadest sense, one might argue that each solution to a problem involves a strategy. Problems can usually be solved either algorithmically or heuristically, and the choice between these could be considered strategic. Moreover, some solutions can be reached in different ways, and again, the choice among these alternatives could be considered strategic. In this broad sense, strategy is coterminous with problem-solving and no further explanation is required. Reassigning the problem to another domain, however, is not a satisfactory resolution.

One possibility for identifying that portion of problem-solving that is strategic is to argue that some kinds of problems can be solved strategically while other kinds of problems are solved through more conventional means that are not strategic. It might be decided, for example, that doing mental arithmetic, learning to read, recalling spatial locations, and memorizing vocabulary lists in a foreign language are problems that involve strategy use, while counting, fluent reading, route tracking, and participating in conversations are problems that do not. Thus, the use of strategies is determined by the type of task. Following this approach, it would then be necessary to set out the conditions that make some problems strategy-based and others not. Yet this, too, cannot provide a satisfactory account of what it means to recruit strategies in the solution to problems. As can be seen with the example of the arithmetic class, different learners approach the same problems in different ways, and some of those approaches involve more effort of a specific kind — planning, decision-making, and the like. A description of strategic behaviour, it seems, will require addressing both the type of problem and the type of solution adopted.

Specifying the features of a solution that may signal the use of strategies is difficult. Brown (1987) has offered: deliberate, goal-directed, tailored to task, consistent, clear relation to performance, and conscious access. She admits, however, that conscious access is dispensable and elsewhere notes a number of apparently complex decision-making processes that may be produced by 'mindless' cognitive activities (Brown and Reeve, 1986). Furthermore, their research shows that age is irrelevant. Strategic approaches to remembering location were observed in children under 2 years of age while adolescent children in school fail to employ the most obvious strategies for studying and recalling information (Brown et al., 1983). Siegler (1987b) rejects almost the entire list, claiming that the only criterion is that the strategy is a cognitively distinct set of activities. Between these extremes, any number of restrictions have been incorporated.

There is little consensus, therefore, on a definitive set of characteristics regarding types of problems or types of solutions that are unequivocally strategic. As will be discussed throughout this volume, the exercise of identifying strategies on the basis of *a priori* features is no more satisfying when applied to the field of second-language communication strategies. Yet, ultimately the issue of identifying strategic behaviour is important in resolving the second issue, namely, the function of such strategies in problem-solving.

Analysis of Strategic Behaviour

The second issue in explaining the use of strategies is to interpret the strategies within some system or explanation of how the problem is solved.

This is essentially the question of how it is that the strategy works, and, perhaps more marginally, why it was selected by that learner. Three current theories of cognitive development will be briefly described to illustrate the kind of explanatory power that can be assigned to the cognitive strategies described above.

The first theory is that proposed by Sternberg (1980). He views intelligence as a function of three component-processes: metacognitive, performance, and knowledge-acquisition. The explanation of strategies resides within the meta-cognitive component. This is the executive and comprises six processes: (1) decide what the problem is, (2) select lower-order components to effect solution, (3) select a strategy for combining lower-order components, (4) select organization of information upon which lower-order components and strategies can act, (5) decide on an appropriate rate for problem-solving, and (6) monitor progress toward solution. This executive, then, contains the cognitive steps which are followed for the child (or adult) to move from understanding a problem situation to achieving a specified goal. Development is characterized by 'greater flexibility and more appropriate strategy or infor-mation utilization ... with age' to reach these goals (Sternberg and Powell, 1983, p. 406). Strategy, in Sternberg's terms, is part of the executive function of problem-solving and operates at the highest level for guiding the solution.

A second cognitive theory built on the notion of strategy use and development comes from the work of Siegler and his colleagues (Siegler and Shrager, 1984; Siegler, 1987a, b). He argues that strategy choice is a central issue in problem-solving. For some tasks, a child could be shown to choose a different strategy to solve the same problem that the child had encountered two weeks earlier, even though there were no differences in processing capacity, availability of strategies, metacognitive knowledge, or content knowledge. The choice of a strategy is responsive to both the child's current state of knowledge and the type of problem being asked. Choosing a strategy, then, is the essence of problem-solving.

Siegler (1987b) distinguishes between solutions which are more or less strategic by introducing a distinction between retrieval strategies and back-up strategies. He defines a back-up strategy 'as any strategy other than retrieval' (p. 2). This definition is not particularly illuminating but the difference becomes more clear through its operationalization in specific problems. Retrieval strategies are fast to use and employed for easy problems; back-up strategies are more accurate and are employed for harder problems. This distinction is reminiscent of the familiar difference between algorithmic and heuristic sol-utions to problems, and the implication is that, for Siegler, both approaches are strategic.

Siegler's model primarily addresses the problem of how a particular strategy is chosen rather than the process description of how the strategies function. Learning is construed as a dynamic process in which the child's representation of a problem changes over time. Each time a child solves a problem, for example, the addition problem $7 + 5$, the strength of the connection between that problem and the correct answer, 12, is modified. The link to 12 is increased in strength and the links to competing incorrect solutions, such as 10, 11, 13, are decreased. Each time the child is confronted with the problem $7 + 5$, the current state of the association to the correct solution, 12, determines the probability that the child will solve the problem using the retrieval strategy. The critical probability value for selecting retrieval, however, is also modified by the problem situation. Under instructions to be fast, a lower threshold would be chosen; under instructions to be accurate, a higher threshold would be used. The model includes three stages which are construed by Siegler to be three sequential processes in solving the problem: retrieval, elaboration of the representation, and use of a back-up strategy (algorithm). Development involves the shift from dependence on back-up strategies to the greater applicability of retrieval strategies.

The third theory comes from the work of Brown and her colleagues (e.g. Brown et al., 1983). The assumption in their programme of research is that there is a qualitative difference between strategic and nonstrategic solutions to problems, and that the strategic approaches can be identified and taught.

Although they do not set out precise criteria for distinguishing strategic from nonstrategic behaviour, they are able to classify solutions in problem situations as being more or less strategic. In their research they have studied children from the age of several months solving simple problems of reaching, locating, and remembering, to teenage children in school struggling with complex academic material. The issue they are interested in is how the strategies of the older or better learner differ from those of the younger or less proficient one. They argue that the advantage to older and more proficient learners accrues from the way in which they have organized their strategies into a coherent system. 'It is the coherence, sturdiness, and resistance to counter suggestion that sets the older child apart from the very young learner. The propensity to be strategic on a variety of learning tasks is much greater' (Brown et al., 1983, p. 95). Moreover, the strategies of the older children are ⎡   ⎤nal' and therefore more generally appropriate to a wider range

4 factors
* *4 characteristics of learner

⎡...⎤ify four factors that determine how a child will solve a problem. ⎡...⎤tors are: (1) learning activities, including attention, rehearsal, ⎡...⎤2) nature of the materials, including physical structure, psycho-⎡...⎤ıre, conceptual difficulty; (3) criterial tasks, such as recognition, ⎡...⎤ı-solving; and (4) characteristics of the learner, including skills, ⎡...⎤ıd attitudes. Strategies are included in the fourth factor as part ⎡...⎤dge base characteristic of the learner. Like any knowledge, the ⎡...⎤ access these strategies and apply them appropriately for their ⎡...⎤ evident; their representation as part of the knowledge base ⎡...⎤arantees for performance.

These three analyses of the role of cognitive strategies in children's problem-solving differ in many ways but converge on two points. First, in all cases strategies are construed as central cognitive elements that are part and parcel of cognitive processing. This is different from interpretations in which a strategy is considered as an option which may be introduced for ornamental or other purposes or is summoned only in special circumstances, such as when difficulties are encountered. Second, in all three theories, strategies are defined by reference to both features of the learner and features of the problem. Description of only one, for example a simple analysis of a solution, is insufficient evidence for the identification and explanation of strategies that might have been used.

Teaching Cognitive Strategies

The third issue is the role of strategies in instructional programmes. Numerous attempts have been made through the years to advance children's progress, particularly in school tasks, by attempting to teach the less successful student the strategies used by their more successful peers. Among these researchers there is a general optimism about the potential for encouraging the use of appropriate strategies through training. Case (1985) muses on how incredibly rapidly children profit from instruction; a small number of trials in a well-designed training session is capable of significantly promoting children to higher levels of problem-solving.

Brown and her colleagues (Brown et al., 1983) have investigated these issues by attempting to determine whether there are general skills (strategies) that apply to a variety of content domains and if so, whether these skills can be taught. Their answer to both is affirmative, and following Butterfield et al. (1973), they conclude that the appropriate educational direction is to explicitly train executive strategies for the selection, sequencing, and co-ordination of more content-specific strategies. The problem, of course, is to develop suitable training methods, and they review a number of approaches, discussing the strengths and weaknesses of each.

In spite of their general optimism concerning the importance and the effectiveness of strategy training for problem-solving, Brown et al. (1983) are careful to point out the limitations as well. Training must take account of the child's initial abilities: what strategies does the child bring to the task? The most effective training simply indicates to the child an occasion in which an existing strategy should be employed. Given the restrictions of memory and executive control that limit the performance of young children, it is conceivable that teaching entirely new strategies is beyond the promise of intervention. Other theorists are more restrained in their expectation for strategy instruction. Training, in Siegler's model, has a limited role, as the child's progress from back-up to retrieval strategies is largely determined by factors internal to the child's cognitive system. The child's representation of the problem, which is the basis of strategy selection, is modified primarily through experience in solving problems of that type. In the mathematical terminology of the model, experience changes the associative strength of the correct response, modifying the likelihood of recruiting a retrieval strategy.

Summary of Cognitive Strategy Research

This brief survey of the strategies used by children to solve cognitive problems has illustrated how each of the three issues of identification, explanation, and instruction contributes to an account of those strategies. Attempts to address each of these issues provide a lesson for the similar endeavours to account for the strategies of communication in a second language.

A definitive set of features that signify the use of a strategy or provide a definition for a strategy has not emerged. None the less, three features of strategies have echoed throughout the various descriptions and appear to apply irrespective of the way that the strategies have been defined, the kinds of problems they have been invoked to solve, and the theoretical explanations constructed for how they work. First, strategies are *effective*: they are related to solutions in specific ways, and they are productive in solving the problem for reasons which theorists can articulate. Second, strategies are *systematic*: learners do not create or stumble upon the best strategy for solving a problem but uncover the strategy from their knowledge of the problem and employ it systematically. Third, strategies are *finite*: a limited number of strategies can be identified. Strategies are not idiosyncratic creations of learners. Larger structures, which some call *executive control structures*, provide a context for organizing strategies into more general skills that are applicable to a range of problems. This systematicity of strategies should be kept as a guiding factor in the search for descriptions and explanations of the strategies used by second-language learners.

Regarding explanations of how strategies work and procedures for training strategies, the most powerful models and most successful programmes follow from positing strategies at the highest levels of cognition. Assigning them executive status in explanations of performance lead to the most fruitful results. Implications for pedagogy follow directly from explanation. Each theory of how strategies work carries its own prescriptions for training.

Communicating is a problem-solving activity and one which requires skilful planning and choice on the part of the speaker. Whatever constrains human information processing to yield the patterns of strategy use observed for children solving problems must also shape the patterns of strategy use observed for adults attempting to communicate.

Explanation of Communication Strategies

It is easy enough to point to examples of speech in which speakers unfamiliar with a language go to great lengths to explain a concept for which they lack a label. But an explanation of communication strategies must do much more than that. The way in which these strategies can be identified (first issue), explained (second issue), and possibly used to modify the behaviour of others (third issue) must be addressed.

An important message to emerge from research on children's cognitive strategies is that definition or illustration is not the same as explanation. An explanation may begin with a definition, but showing how a system works requires another level of analysis. Thus, explanations of the communication strategies of second-language learners must go beyond the descriptions and illustrations that have been used in the first step to identify them. Training in the use of effective strategies, as was shown in the research with children, followed most successfully from explanatory models that related the operation of the relevant strategies to other high-level cognitive processes.

The goal of the analysis of communication strategies that is developed in this volume is to find a means of explaining how strategies function in the speech of second-language learners. A different goal would have led to a different kind of analysis from the one pursued here. The goal of explaining the linguistic devices that are used to realize strategies, for example, would direct greater attention to the linguistic forms. The goal of explaining the social interactions that surround communication would direct greater attention to the interpersonal aspects of communication. But the purpose of the present inquiry is to discover what communication strategies are, who uses them and for what reasons, and how they are developed either through ordinary language acquisition or special instruction. The inquiry begins with the first issue: how can we identify communication strategies?

2 Identifying Communication Strategies

It is easy to decide that speakers engage in a variety of strategies in order to communicate. It is not easy to decide how to identify when strategies have been used, what the strategies are, and why it is that they work (or don't work). To what extent is language use − in particular, communication − *strategic*? What are the boundaries between what we might consider to be ordinary communication and strategic communication? Are the boundaries different when one is speaking in a first or second language?

Communication is not the only domain of language use that invites strategic behaviour. Learning a second language, understanding spoken language beyond one's formal proficiency level, achieving pragmatic goals with a second language in appropriate ways may all be considered strategic in that the speaker/learner has to make some choices about how to achieve the goal. Even within second-language use, therefore, there are many questions regarding the delineation of strategy use.

The concern in this chapter is to examine various ways of defining strategic behaviour for second-language learners. The discussion will begin at the broadest level of inquiry and gradually narrow the focus until specific communication strategies are the topic. Accordingly, the first section will discuss the distinction between *strategies* of learning or communication and the corresponding *processes* underlying language learning and use. If strategies and processes are different types of events, then the critical differences must be identified. The second section will consider different language functions (uses) that may be served by strategies. The primary division that will be considered is between strategies of *learning* and strategies of *communication*. The third section will focus on one of these uses, namely, communication, and present a classification of *types of communication strategies*. This organization assumes a hierarchical structure as can be seen in figure 2.1.

Distinguishing Strategies from other Events

Is all language use strategic? If the concept of strategies has any special meaning, then the distinction between strategic and nonstrategic language use

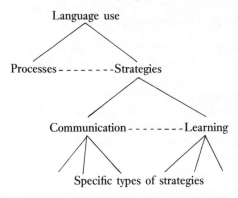

Figure 2.1

must be determined. Further, if a distinction between strategic and nonstrategic language use is to be maintained, then a different description is required for how each works for second-language learners. A distinction between these two types of systems must be defended by demonstrating the way in which strategic language use proceeds differently from nonstrategic language use. Accordingly, before one begins to describe how strategies work, it is necessary to identify what the alternatives are. What is in control of language when it is *not* strategic?

One conceptual distinction which reflects this difference is that between *strategy* and *process*. Process is generally used in psychology to refer to the mental steps taken to carry out a cognitive activity. Processes can be completely unconscious and inaccessible to the individual, such as the visual processes that allow us to recognize faces, judge distances, and read text. Other processes operate at a higher level and are more amenable to inspection and modification, such as the computational processes that allow us to add a column of numbers or follow a route on a map. Mental processes of both these kinds control communication as well: relatively unconscious processes are responsible for generating well-formed utterances according to the rules of grammar, while more conscious processes are involved in monitoring the conversation and determining the intentional content of utterances. But the claim for a role for strategies requires more. For carrying on a conversation, for example, it would also be the case that part of our use of language for that purpose was additionally or alternatively under the control of specialized communication strategies. The same case could be made for learning. Although learning a language involves a large number of relatively unconscious processes — we do not really know why reading a passage has the effect of somehow expanding our knowledge of the language — the procedure can be mediated by activities we introduce for the purpose of learning. These strategies would include the various techniques we adopt to help us remember new material. A number of criteria have been suggested to distinguish between the strategies and processes of language learning and use.

Time Constraints on Strategy

Blum and Levenston (1978) use the dimension of temporality to discriminate strategy from process. Strategies, in their view, are 'the way the learner arrives at a certain usage at a specific point in time' (p. 402). Strategies, then, are isolated occurrences manifested on a single occasion. Thus, a learner may use a strategy of simplification to solve a unique problem confronted at that moment. For example, lacking the correct word for *rose*, the second-language learner may comment on the pretty *flowers* in the vase. This would be the *strategy of simplification*.

Over time, the repeated occurrence of such instances can lead to an internal change in the organization of the second language. The term *flower* is incorporated as the usual word for reference to roses, and the learner's interlanguage becomes simplified. This is the *process of simplification*. Blum and Levenston define this process as 'the systematic series of steps by which the learner arrives at the same usage over time' (1978, p. 402).

The important feature of their analysis is that they propose a hierarchically ordered relation among three events: performance, strategies, and processes. The available data are confined to observable performance, but each level of analysis is sequentially deducible from the previous one. Thus, examination of the learner's utterances allows one to infer the strategies motivating those utterances, and overall examination of strategies over time leads to higher-order inferences about processes. In this way, the processes of second-language use are a level of analysis distinct from strategies or from pure performance, although their description of such processes is necessarily more indirect. These relations might be represented as follows:

In Blum and Levenston's conceptualization, there are two possible outcomes once a strategy has been used in performance. One is that the strategy (e.g. simplifying a term to solve a problem at this moment) may become incorporated into the interlanguage by the corresponding process (e.g. simplification in which the second-language vocabulary is adjusted to use only the simplified term). Alternatively, the strategy may be used on the single occasion then disappear, having served its purpose in a momentary communication problem. These alternatives form the basis of a distinction they propose between two kinds of strategies: strategies that can *initiate processes* and strategies that are *situation bound*. These types of strategies are shown in table 2.1. It is only the process-initiating strategies that have an influence on the development of the learner's interlanguage. For this reason, these process-initiating strategies might be equivalent to what others have called *learning strategies* (discussed in the next section of this chapter). The situation-bound strategies, however, function more as the typical *communication strategy* of other systems (discussed in detail in chapter 3).

Table 2.1 Communication strategies of lexical simplification

Group A: *Potentially process initiating*
1 Overgeneralization realized by:
    a the use of superordinate terms
    b approximation
    c the use of synonymy
    d word coinage
    e the use of converse terms
2 Transfer

Group B: *Situation bound*
1 Circumlocution and paraphrase
2 Language switch
3 Appeal to authority
4 Change of topic
5 Semantic avoidance

Source: From S. Blum-Kulka and E. Levenston, Universals of lexical simplification, p. 126. In C. Faerch and G. Kasper (eds), *Strategies in Interlanguage Communication*. Copyright Longman 1983. Reprinted by permission.

Blum and Levenston's suggested method of demarcating strategies in this way is interesting. The assumption is not only that strategies and processes are different types of events, but also that there exists a systematic relation between them which can be defined on a given dimension. Strategies and processes are interconnected in an explanation of second-language use.

A similar distinction is proposed by Seliger (1984). In an attempt to model the processes involved in second-language acquisition, he posits a constrast between *strategy* and *tactic*. Strategies are 'universal, age- and context-independent, and when engaged must be assumed to lead to long-term acquisition' (p. 38). Tactics are devices used to meet the immediate demands of a situation and are 'dependent on a wide variety of factors such as environment, age, personality, affective constraints, and first language' (p. 38). He also uses differences in consciousness to distinguish strategy from tactic, claiming that strategies are unconscious and inaccessible to inspection. Although the implications of Seliger's distinction are much broader for a theory of acquisition than those that follow from the Blum and Levenston model, the two theories converge on distinguishing between linguistic processes that are ongoing over long periods of time and those that are momentary solutions to a current situation.

Seliger's intention in making this distinction is to suggest a means for describing the universal aspects of second-language acquisition that determine the similarities in the process across enormous variations in context, purpose, and individual characteristics. The level of tactic in this model more or less corresponds to the level most theories have reserved for strategy, while strategy is elevated to a higher-level cognitive process. It will be argued in chapter 7 that Seliger is correct in attempting to place the explanatory burden at the universal level, leaving the situation-specific behaviour a matter of superficial variation. However, the criterion by which he makes the distinction, namely, temporality, is problematic.

The proposals to discriminate between strategy and process are sensible and lead to a rational means for relating strategy and process, but the use of temporality as the deciding criterion presents some difficulties with the analysis. The main problem is that the critical dimension which serves to distinguish strategies from processes lacks objective measure. Processes are inferred to have occurred if the effects of strategies are observed over time. But what are the temporal boundaries that classify the use of a simplification, for example, as a strategy or a process? Is a day too long? Is one conversation too short? What if the strategy/process recurs at regular intervals but is not consistently evident in that the learner's speech fluctuates among different terms for that concept? The relevant difference seems more to be the consistency with which the strategies are observed over time as evidenced by changes in the learner's interlanguage. Temporality seems too precarious a criterion to critically distinguish between these constructs.

The second problem is a corollary of the first. Because the distinction between strategy and process is determined temporally, the two events overlap. The risk is that both strategy and process are being used to describe the same behaviour but at different levels of analysis — one synchronically (strategies) and the other diachronically (processes). The same performance, that is, can be interpreted as a strategy if it is examined at a single point in time for a single concept, or as a process if it is examined over long periods of time for larger semantic domains. For this reason, the distinction captures a difference in description and analysis but not necessarily a difference in language use. In this way, any process observed at a single point in time could be called a strategy and any strategy observed with sufficient (but undetermined) frequency could be called a process. Thus the constructs are reduced to methodological variants.

Strategies as Options

Another criterion for distinguishing strategies from processes is the extent to which the behaviour is optional in a given context (Bialystok, 1978; Frauenfelder and Porquier, 1979). The idea originally motivating this criterion was that there is level of performance which is the inevitable, perhaps automatic, mental functioning of the linguistic system. These processes are carried out by a mental executive (some control structure that oversees all performance) in response to the demands of the problem under the constraints of the system (including knowledge of the target language, knowledge of other languages, and conceptual knowledge as well as processing abilities). This is a standard interpretation of cognitive performance in information-processing psychology (see the discussion of Sternberg's model of problem-solving in chapter 1). An additional construct is necessary only when the learner/performer intercedes in these usual processes to change the normal routine, and hence, the expected form of response. To this end, strategies are defined as supplementary activities that the learner can impose on the autonomous system to expedite achieving a goal.

Using this criterion of optionality, the Monitor hypothesized by Krashen (1981) is an example of strategy. In Krashen's description, the Monitor is a supplementary system invoked at the will of the learner to modify performance. Accordingly, the use of the Monitor is a choice that is at the discretion of the speaker. The main problem with Krashen's analysis is that he insists on isolating the Monitor from other language processes. If an auxiliary system such as a monitor contributes to an overall performance, then there must be interfaces among the systems and means for sharing resources such as knowledge. In the absence of such co-operation, the Monitor functions as an autonomous system in itself and it is difficult to imagine how any coherent behaviour could be produced. An excellent critique of Krashen's work is presented by McLaughlin (1987).

The criterion of optionality sets out another means for establishing the ways in which strategies are different from processes. The learner's strategic intervention in the usual processes governing language production presumably leads to observably distinct forms of behaviour. Thus, an examination of the form of speech produced by a learner should indicate whether or not that speech was the result of normal production processes or had been shaped as well by communication (or other) strategies. Contrary to the previous system in which the level of analysis determined whether the same behaviour should be described as the result of a strategy or a process, in this system the behaviour itself is different if its initiation is attributed to production processes or communication strategies. Strategies, that is, should reliably produce forms of language that are different from those that one would expect to emanate from the autonomous processing system. Documentation of these forms would enable one to detect the strategic intervention of the language learner. This system might be diagrammed as follows:

$$\text{Process} \longrightarrow \text{Product 1}$$
$$\text{Process} - (+ \text{ Strategy}) \longrightarrow \text{Product 2}$$

But how does the examination of speech betray the presence of strategies? Presumably one could compare the observed speech performance with speech production that would be expected as the *norm*, that is, performance in the absence of strategies. But how could such norms be established? Strategies, then, mark deviance from the language produced under normal conditions of language processing. Yet the implication that language production under the guidance of strategies is somehow less normal than that under usual processing conditions seems to be incorrect. Further, in this view, strategies would entail active intervention by the learner. The implicit criteria for strategies would logically include such features as purposeful and deliberate acts by the learner. In view of the review of the definitions of strategies presented in chapter 1, these criteria may not be correct.

Planning Strategies and the Strategy of Planning

A third attempt to set strategies of communication apart from other theoretical constructs is the distinction between strategies and plans offered by Faerch and Kasper (1983a). The distinction is made within the context of a broad model of language production. The model consists of two phases: a *planning phase* and an *execution phase*. Thus separate processing steps are assigned to the learner's preparation for communication and to the actual communication which ensues. The result of the first phase is the formulation of a plan to achieve the communicative goal; the result of the second is the execution of that plan, that is, observable speech. Faerch and Kasper argue that strategies are relevant only to the planning phase.

Both planning and execution, according to Faerch and Kasper, involve processes. Execution, in their view, is under the control of neurological and physiological processes which are both more trivial and less observable than the processes that control the planning phase.[1] It is in the planning phase that the 'language user selects rules and items which he considers most appropriate for establishing a plan, the execution of which will lead to verbal behaviour which is expected to satisfy the original goal' (Faerch and Kasper, 1983a, p. 25). Moreover, this planning process is 'normally subconscious and highly automatic' for first language (L1) production.

In this system, process is defined at a high level and determines the functioning of each of the planning and execution phases. Thus, Faerch and Kasper point out that the real opposition for process is not strategy, but product. They choose a broad interpretation for process and adopt definitions from Brown (1976, p. 136): process is 'continuing development involving a number of changes' and Klaus and Buhr (1976, p. 990, cited in Faerch and Kasper, 1983a, p. 30): 'a dynamic sequence of different stages of an object or system'. Thus they include as equivalent such applications as 'the process of L2 acquisition', 'the communication process', and the 'restructuring and recreation processes'.

Defined in such broad terms, strategies cannot be equivalent to processes,

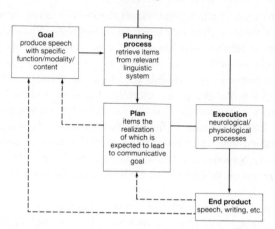

Figure 2.2 Model of speech production. From C. Faerch and G. Kasper, Plans and
strategies in foreign language communication, p. 25. In C. Faerch and G.
Kasper (eds), *Strategies in Interlanguage Communication.* Copyright
Longman 1983. Reprinted by permission.

nor can they exist at a similar level of analysis as processes. The comparable
constructs to strategies for Faerch and Kasper, rather, are plans. They define
communication strategies as special plans that are developed during the
planning phase as part of the planning process. These strategies become
involved in the formation of a communicative plan during some process of
preparing speech. Strategies, then, are a subclass of plans. A diagram of one
form of their model is reproduced in figure 2.2.

The system they propose in this framework is hierarchical – strategies are
incorporated into plans, and plans form one of the two essential processes of
communication, namely, the planning process. Further, strategies are given
the defining criteria of *problem-orientedness* and *consciousness.* Strategies, in this
view, are those plans which are developed in response to a problem through
the conscious intervention of the speaker. They are therefore supplemental to
communication in that they are an extra step that may be inserted into
production when a problem arises. To what extent does this conceptualization
succeed in setting out precise boundaries for distinguishing between strategies
and other related events, especially processes?

The system proposed by Faerch and Kasper is an ambitious attempt to
sketch out a model of speech production, more specifically, speech production
in a second language. In the first stage of such model-building it is necessary
to accumulate all the relevant mechanisms that will impinge on the system. To
this end, Faerch and Kasper have contributed the most complete model of
communication strategies by placing them in a comprehensive theoretical
description of speech production. Included in their model are the role of such
relevant factors as the communicative goal, representation of linguistic (and
presumably other kinds of) knowledge, neurological and physiological speech

production processes, monitoring systems to establish correctness and fluency, and the like. Moreover, their insistence on distinguishing between process and product is an important clarification of two concepts that are frequently confused in other models.

The second step of model building is to assign precise definitions to the mechanisms in the model and to determine the nature of their interaction in order to assess the psychological reality or even the psychological plausibility of the model. The interaction of the mechanisms depends to a great extent on the definitions that have been assigned. It is on this issue of definition that the Faerch and Kasper model is weak, and as a result of some uncertainty in their definition of terms, it is difficult to envisage how the model would be made operational.

The success of the model depends on the definitions of the basic concepts, namely *process*, *plan*, and *strategy*. Although Faerch and Kasper insist that communication strategies should not be considered as a subclass of processes, their description of speech production clearly places *process* at a higher level of analysis than *plan* or *strategy*, inviting vertical ordering. At the same time, they argue that strategies are outside of the execution process in that they 'steer, monitor, or control speech execution'. Yet how would one separate such a monitoring function for execution from the execution itself? It is difficult to imagine how such monitoring could be outside the system (or 'processing phase', in their terms).

Crucial to this model is the distinction between the planning and execution phases. Yet this distinction is the most difficult aspect of the model to demonstrate both theoretically (using, for example, precise definitions) or empirically. It is not even clear what sort of evidence would support this dichotomy as a valid distinction. Such distinctions are not new. Clark and Clark (1977) used a similar pair of concepts for their interpretation of language production but went on to caution against applying the distinction too rigorously: 'The division between planning and execution, however, is not a clear one. At any moment speakers are usually doing a little of both ... It is impossible to say where planning leaves off and execution begins' (Clark and Clark, 1977, p. 224). The solution adopted by Clark and Clark is to consider planning and execution as the endpoints of five steps in speech production. Intervening steps gradually fade from planning to execution. The five steps are: discourse plans, sentence plans, constituent plans, articulatory programme, and articulation.

A similar problem has been encountered in the field of memory research in which theoretical models of memory rested on a distinction analogous to that between planning and execution for language production. For memory research, the relevant division is between storage (cf. planning) and retrieval (cf. execution). It is only recently that researchers have made any progress with this problem through the clinical studies of amnesiacs. Neuropsychological evidence for distinct storage and retrieval processes is still ambiguous.

The distinction between planning and execution may be entirely correct, but at this point in time, substantiating evidence is precarious. In general, without more convincing evidence to show that planning and execution are separate, it is difficult to see how this distinction would be applied in the model of second-language production.

Criteria for Identifying Strategies

The three approaches examined here have all attempted to identify critical parameters that could reliably lead to decisions regarding the respective roles for strategies and process in communicative language production. Blum and Levenston, and Seliger, distinguished strategy from process by evaluating temporal conditions; Bialystok, and Frauenfelder and Porquier, distinguished strategy from process by considering the optionality of the event; and Faerch and Kasper set aside processes as referring to events at a different level of analysis, then distinguished strategy from plan in terms of the problem-relatedness and consciousness of the event. An adequate description of strategies that would clearly distinguish them from other constructs would need to meet two criteria: behavioural evidence and objective measure. Each of the attempts described above fails to satisfy one or both of these criteria.

The first criterion is behavioural evidence. If we are to assume that strategies and processes are unique systems underlying production, then there must be distinct non-overlapping evidence for the existence of each. This is not to say that processes, or even strategies, need to be directly observable. On the contrary, the most interesting cognitive phenomena can never be observed directly, but at the same time manifestations of those phenomena are clear. Cognitive psychologists, for example, often posit a distinction between long-term memory and short-term memory. Evidence for their separate existence is that each system is specialized for the retrieval of different information. Long-term memory is organized into categories and operates over long periods of time, perhaps permanently; short-term memory is organized temporally, operates from surface forms (such as phonology) and lasts only briefly. Thus, although the two memory systems are not accessible to direct inspection, evidence from memory behaviour attests to their separate responsibilities. People reliably recall in different ways as a function of the elapsed time. Similarly for communication, if strategies and processes are distinct constructs, we would expect to see qualitative differences in behaviour that could be attributed to the presence of each system.

The approach that has come closest to meeting this criterion is that of Faerch and Kasper. In their terminology, the relevant contrast to strategy is not process, but plan. None the less, they clearly understand the problem, and claim that the: 'central task ... is to find out whether there are specific features of performance which unambiguously indicate that the planning/execution process leading to this performance has been strategic' (1983b, p. 213). They offer three types of performance features as evidence for strategic intervention: temporal variables, such as rate of articulation pauses, drawls, and repeats; self-repairs, such as false starts and new starts; and speech slips, such as lapses and speech errors.

These indications may well signal strategic intervention, but it is not inevitable that they do. These criteria further present the possibility that strategies are confined to instances of speech errors, a consequence which would seem to contradict Faerch and Kasper's argument that strategies exist in the planning phase. Equating strategies with speech errors of this type would also trivialize the construct, including only such performance errors that could be detected by superficial linguistic analysis. Accordingly, one would have to allow that these performance features may indicate strategic intervention on some occasions, but that strategies may well have motivated utterances that occur in the absence of such features. Similarly, the presence of such performance features may be related to such phenomena as attention gaps, change of intention, and other forms of distraction, none of which are notably strategic.

The second criterion for distinguishing between strategies and processes is that the parameter is objective and can be reliably applied to new situations. Here most of the approaches suffer. In the Blum and Levenston approach, it is impossible to tell from a single speech sample whether communication is being governed by a strategy or a process — only intimate knowledge of the speaker could yield that information. Is a strategy rigidly restricted to one occurrence before it becomes a process or will six or seven isolated instances remain strategic? The parameter of optionality is no better. Judgements of strategic behaviour based on the optionality of the response would theoretically require that the researcher had access to all possible responses so that the optimal utterance, presumably the one generated by the process, could be determined. It also has the unfortunate corollary of implying that communication is possible without any intervention or choice at all by the speaker. Normal conversation which emerges from the process of communicating would proceed with little or no interference from the speaker! Finally, the third position uses the objective criterion of problematicity in the communicative situation. Identifying strategic situations, then, requires that researchers are aware of the mental states of language learners when they produce specific utterances. Problems can certainly be assumed to exist when there are overt signs such as pauses, errors, false starts, and the like, but they undoubtedly also occur even when there is no external evidence to betray them.

How, then, to distinguish strategies of communication from the process of communicating (or, for Faerch and Kasper, for communicative plans)? It is clear that second-language learners struggle to communicate in a way that is not necessary when communicating in one's native language. It is also clear that there is much systematicity in these attempts, both in the process of generating the communication and in the product that results, namely, the kinds of errors and alternatives language learners routinely use. But attempts to define the criteria by which communication can be attributed to strategic intervention have been fragile. No criterion proposed thus far has managed to indicate the special part of language production that is properly strategic.

Strategies may yet prove to constitute a unique aspect of the language production system, but their proper description has not been established through these means. Without substantial direction in how to proceed with a distinction between strategies and process of language production, the possibility that these are ultimately not different events remains tenable.

Types of Strategies in Language Use

A different means of trying to apprehend the construct of communication strategies is to distinguish them, not from processes, but from other sorts of strategies implicated in second-language use. This approach is more functional in that performance is first examined and then assigned to descriptive categories. This inductive approach may prove more fruitful than the deductive approach implicit in the attempt to establish a reliable definition *a priori*.

Strategies can be used for a range of goals, only one of which is communication. The second problem, then, is to identify the domain of strategies occurring in second-language use and assign to them a unique role in learning and performance. Unlike the first issue, which was an attempt to distinguish communication strategies from communication processes, the attempt in this case is to identify varieties of strategies. The task should be simpler, as behavioural criteria that signify different forms of mental states are not necessary. The task, that is, can be approached directly through the examination of learner performance.

Strategies in Interlanguage

The first systematic attempt to set out the broad domain of strategies and indicate its subclasses is the description of interlanguage introduced by Selinker (1972). In that seminal work, he identifies five *processes* in the development of interlanguage: language transfer, overgeneralization of target language rules, transfer of training, strategies of second-language (L2) learning, and strategies of L2 communication. These five processes jointly bear responsibility for the movement of the interlanguage along some hypothetical continuum towards the norms set out by the target language. The two strategies (pertaining to learning and communication) enjoy equal status with the other processes, and the evaluative criteria in all cases are not some theoretical psychological system, but measurable differences in the form of the interlanguage as a function of these factors. Thus, Selinker would claim that there is no important distinction between strategies and processes, but that strategies simply comprise some of the relevant language acquisition processes. In the interlanguage view, strategies of learning need to be distinguished only from strategies of communication.

Language Use versus Language Learning

The original proposals regarding the definition and function of strategies proposed by Selinker were developed and greatly explicated in a major research programme by Tarone (1977, 1979, 1980). In addition to her methodological and taxonomical contributions (which will be discussed in chapter 3), she provides an important theoretical context for studying the problem of strategies and offers explicit definitions for distinguishing between the different kinds of strategies used by second-language learners (Tarone, 1980).

Following Selinker, Tarone first distinguishes between strategies of language use and language-learning strategies. The former contains two subcategories: *communication strategies* and *production strategies*. She defines communication strategies as 'a mutual attempt of two interlocutors to agree on a meaning in situations where requisite meaning structures do not seem to be shared' and production strategies as 'an attempt to use one's linguistic system efficiently and clearly, with a minimum of effort'. The difference between these two is the effort of the speaker to consider the effect of the utterance on an interlocutor. In this way, communication strategies apply only to language in its interactive form, and necessarily involve sociolinguistic as well as the usual linguistic and psycholinguistic considerations. It is an important point, and one rarely made in analyses of communication strategies.

Language-learning strategies were defined by Tarone as 'an attempt to develop linguistic and sociolinguistic competence in the target language'. She included in this category all the usual pedagogical activities that have the express purpose of assisting memory and providing practice. Some of her examples are memorization, repetition with purpose of remembering, mnemonics, initiation of conversation with native speakers, inferencing, and spelling. This type of strategy is perhaps best construed as a specialized subset of the normal learning activities that can be applied to any content domain.

Productive Strategies

Corder (1983) also addressed the problem of identifying types of strategies used by second-language learners. He makes the important point that all speakers adopt strategies but that they are simply more apparent for non-native speakers. This is an issue which sometimes gets lost in the attempt to describe the speech of second-language learners, but one which will be echoed throughout this volume.

The major distinction Corder proposes is one between *productive strategies* and *receptive strategies*. He observed that there is an asymmetry between these two in the amount of research attention they have received, the larger portion being assigned to production strategies. In second-language acquisition, some important work in reception strategies has been carried out by Bates and her colleagues (Bates et al., 1982) but, as Corder points out, research in the area is sparse. First-language acquisition also suffers from the disproportionate attention paid to speech production at the expense of the receptive aspects of language use. The notable contributions to literature on speech reception in first-language processing are Slobin's (1973) operating principles and Garrett et al.'s (1965) segmentation studies.

The main point of Corder's discussion is his interpretation of the difference between learning strategies and communication strategies, both productive strategies in his terms. This classification is a departure from Tarone's, in which learning strategies were set apart from the two productive strategies, production and communication. Corder, that is, puts together two types of strategies which for Tarone were categorically different. Yet he argues that it is difficult (if at all possible) to classify language data as belonging simply to one or the other category, namely, to strategies of communication or strategies of language use. Is the insertion of an L1 term, for example, the result of a learning strategy to transfer L1 items to supplement an incomplete interlanguage or the result of a communication strategy to borrow from the L1 in an effort to solve an immediate problem? To further complicate the issue, such strategies operating as communication strategies, that is, borrowing in the service of acute communicative difficulty, can none the less lead to learning. Such examples abound. What of the strategy of memorizing a short routine that will be needed on a specific occasion, such as memorizing the form needed to enter a bakery and obtain a loaf of bread and two rolls? Memorizing is a classic learning strategy (see Stern, 1983), but it is used in this case for a specific communicative function, and quite possibly forgotten as soon as the bread and rolls have become a memory. Such examples support Corder's view that simple classifications of learner strategies into types on the basis of their function for the learner are facile.

Learning Strategies

While *a priori* classification of strategies into types or groups according to their function has not always been successful, descriptions of specific strategies have been more informative. Motivated by an interest in language teaching theory, Stern (1983) presented a comprehensive discussion of the strategies of second-language learners. His primary interest was in learning strategies, but his analysis offers clear direction as to how communication strategies might be interpreted. Stern's conceptualization is built from earlier lists of learning strategies offered by both himself (Stern, 1975) and others (Rubin, 1975; Naiman et al., 1978; Hosenfeld, 1979). From these lists, he develops an interesting and plausible view of what these strategies represent and how they contribute to learning.

Stern observed that the term 'strategy' has been used inconsistently, and offers the definition that learning strategies refer to: 'general tendencies or overall characteristics of the approach employed by the language learner, leaving learning techniques as the term to refer to particular forms of observable learning behaviour, more or less consciously employed by the learner' (1983,

p. 405). Thus, strategies are construed at a relatively high level of analysis, embracing a number of instantiations of the strategy. Moreover, it appears that these strategies each represent some conscious choice by the learner, although the specific manifestation of the strategy may be less intentional.

In this way, Stern identifies four strategies, the use of which possibly distinguishes successful from unsuccessful language learners. First is the *active planning strategy*. Good language learners actively participate in their learning process by selecting goals, recognizing stages, and the like. Second is the *academic (explicit) learning strategy*. This is the strategy in which learners approach a language as an academic problem, a structured body of knowledge which needs to be learned. Third is the *social learning strategy*. In this strategy, language learners seek opportunities to use the second language through any available means: conversations, books, films, and the like. Moreover, good language learners 'will tend to develop and use "communication strategies", i.e., techniques of coping with difficulties in communicating in an imperfectly known second language' (p. 411). Fourth is the *affective strategy*. This strategy is a means of coping with the emotional and motivational problems that inevitably accompany second-language learning. The remedy is generally the cultivation of positive attitudes towards the self, the language, and the society and culture it represents.

Stern's analysis is a significantly different way of conceptualizing the strategies of second-language learners. There is no attempt to classify strategies as belonging to the domain of learning or communication. Such a classificatory approach is obviated by Stern's integrated view of language learning. He claims that there are four characteristics of language proficiency: formal mastery, semantic mastery, communicative capacity, and creativity, and that these 'are best assumed to develop simultaneously from the start, and to complement each other throughout the learning process' (p. 400). In this way, distinctions between learning and communication become vacuous. Communication strategies, rather, are one set of special techniques that learners employ as part of the learning strategy of social integration.

Social Strategies

A different sort of distinction, but one which is none the less relevant to communication, is made by Wong Fillmore (1979). She points out that the initial problem in second-language acquisition is to master a set of 'social strategies' so that contact and input become possible. She identifies three social strategies and connects them to a set of cognitive strategies that capitalize on the created opportunities and allow the language learner to progress with communication and language learning. These strategies are reproduced in table 2.2.

The advice in this list perhaps comes the closest to a direct order to use communication strategies is C-4: 'Make the most of what you've got'. This recommendation assumes that communication can proceed from an incomplete linguistic system and that such efforts are advantageous to the learner. Both of

Table 2.2   Social and cognitive strategies

Social strategies	Cognitive strategies
S-1: Join a group and act as if you understand what's going on, even if you don't	C-1: Assume that what people are saying is directly relevant to the situation at hand, or to what they or you are experiencing. Guess!
S-2: Give the impression – with a few well-chosen words – that you can speak the language	C-2: Get some expressions you understand and start talking
S-3: Count on your friends for help	C-3: Look for recurring parts in the formulas you know
	C-4: Make the most of what you've got
	C-5: Work on the big things first; save the details for later

Source: L. Wong Fillmore, Individual differences in second language acquisition. In C. J. Fillmore, D. Kempler and W. S.-Y. Wong (eds), *Individual Differences in Language Ability and Language Behavior.* Copyright Academic Press 1979. Reprinted by permission.

these assumptions are surely correct. The language produced by children applying these strategies is not very different from the sorts of utterances that are usually the object of study for communication strategies. Some children she observed avoided topics, and others used 'semantic extension' as a means of referring to objects they could not label. One example is a child who used 'sangwish' to refer to all food.

Wong Fillmore goes on to argue that differences in the use of these strategies account for important individual differences in the success with which children learn a second language. She attributes these individual differences to: 'the nature of the task, the set of strategies they needed to apply in dealing with it, and the way certain personal characteristics such as language habits, motivations, social needs and habitual approaches to problems affected the way they attacked it' (p. 220). In this view, communication strategies are traced to a set of social and cognitive strategies that control the way in which children will interact with the target language and the benefit that might accrue from that interaction.

Classifying Communication Strategies

The third step in identifying the domain of behaviour that constitutes communication strategies is to examine systematic differences among different types of communication strategies. Are there reliable features which organize the variety of communication strategies along linguistic, psycholinguistic, or contextual lines?

Message Adjustment versus Resource Expansion

Corder (1983) sets out a productive means of assigning communication strategies to different types. In one way or another, his criterion permeates most descriptive systems developed for this purpose. The distinction is based on a metaphor for language production in which speakers hold an intended meaning, or goal, in mind, and select a route to that goal from some repertoire. When the mechanism fails to provide a route to that goal, the possibilities are either to change the goal to one for which a route is possible, or to change the route to that same goal, using one that is less optimal. Children learning their first language routinely encounter the same problem as they frequently wish to make reference to objects and events for which they lack the correct label. Their usual choice is to change the goal, settling for a reference to an object or event which is similar but not identical to their intended meaning, but is lexically available in their knowledge of the language. Children's communicative use of their first language will be discussed in chapter 5.

The instantiations of the two options for second-language communication into specific communication strategies are either to tailor the message to come into congruence with the linguistic resources of the speaker, or to increase, extend, or manipulate the available linguistic system so that it becomes capable of realizing the intended message. Corder calls the strategies produced by the first option *message adjustment strategies* and those by the second, *resource expansion strategies*.

The extent to which the speaker compromises the original goal when using the message adjustment strategies is scaled on a dimension of globalness. Entire topics can be avoided, specific meanings within topics can be abandoned, a finite set of semantic relations can be avoided, or given messages can simply be reduced, retaining some but not all of the features originally intended. This ordering is the sequence of most global to least global (most local) strategies.

Resource expansion strategies can be scaled in terms of their inducement of risk-taking by the speaker. All such strategies involve some risk to the speaker who must extend the available linguistic resources. Accordingly, these strategies are associated with a high probability of error. The scale of risk-taking indicates the extent to which the speaker is risking communication failure. Switching languages is the least effective means of guaranteeing comprehension of a target-language listener and therefore carries the greatest risk of failure. Paraphrasing intentions is more likely to be successful, and the use of paralinguistic features may be less communicatively efficient but involves the least risk. This ordering, then, scales the strategies from the most risk-taking to the least risk-taking. The specific varieties of these risk-taking strategies are the ones usually identified in taxonomies of communication strategies and will be discussed further in chapter 3.

Reduction Strategies versus Achievement Strategies

Faerch and Kasper (1983a) propose a system for classifying communication strategies that sets out types of strategies on a basis reminiscent of the one suggested by Corder. They argue that learners facing a communication problem have a choice between two approaches: they can dismiss the problem by circumventing the difficulty (cf. message adjustment strategies), thus *avoiding* the obstacle, or they can confront the problem by developing an alternative plan (cf. resource expansion strategies), thus *achieving* a solution. This choice represents the major division in their classification, that between *reduction strategies* on the one hand, which follow from avoidance of difficulty, and *achievement strategies* on the other, which follow from attempts to conquer the problem. The choice between these approaches depends on the learner's underlying behaviour being avoidance-oriented or achievement-oriented, and on the nature of the encountered problem. An overview of these strategy types is shown in table 2.3.

Reduction strategies are further divided into two types: formal reduction strategies and functional reduction strategies. Formal reduction strategies, in fact, do not fit well into the classification and they are assigned special status. These strategies are the attempts by the learner to avoid errors by generating speech production from a reduced system. The assumption is that the rules, structures, or items are present in the learner's interlanguage system, but the speaker chooses not to use them.

Table 2.3 Overview of communication strategies

Formal reduction strategies Learner communicates by means of a 'reduced' system, in order to avoid producing nonfluent or incorrect utterances by realizing insufficiently automatized or hypothetical rules/items	*Subtypes* phonological morphological syntactic lexical
Functional reduction strategies Learner reduces his communicative goal in order to avoid a problem	*Subtypes* actional reduction modal reduction reduction of propositional content
Achievement strategies Learner attempts to solve a problem by expanding his communicative resources	*Subtypes* compensatory strategy a code switch b transfer c interlanguage-based strategies d co-operative e nonlinguistic

Source: From C. Faerch and G. Kasper, Plans and strategies in foreign language communication, pp. 52–3. In C. Faerch and G. Kasper (eds), *Strategies in Interlanguage Communication.* Copyright Longman 1983. Reprinted by permission.

Two reasons are suggested for this avoidance that characterizes formal reduction. First, the learner could be attempting to avoid errors because the structures are difficult or their representation in the learner's linguistic system is not clear. Second, the learner could be attempting to increase fluency by avoiding items that are not sufficiently automatized or easily retrievable. These possibilities correspond to the basic difference set out between avoidance strategies and achievement strategies. In the case of avoiding errors, the learner is avoiding; in the case of increasing fluency, the learner is achieving. Hence, formal reduction occurs as both strategy types.

Functional reduction strategies are generated in response to problems in either the planning phase or execution phase. They occur when linguistic resources are lacking (i.e. the route to the goal is not available), or cannot be accessed (retrieval problem). Functional reduction strategies are those solutions which involve reducing, avoiding, or abandoning the original communicative goal.

The type of communication strategy into which Faerch and Kasper invest the most promise is achievement strategies. These are the compensatory strategies that are developed in the planning phase to overcome the lack of an available route to the communicative goal. They are based on information from a variety of sources: the L1 code, the interlanguage code, discourse rules, and nonlinguistic features. These are the strategies which receive most of the attention in taxonomies of second-language communication discussed in chapter 3.

Adjusted Meaning versus Adjusted Form

The contrast between adjusting the meaning and adjusting the form of expression is also the basis of the system set out by Varadi (1980). His scheme is more differentiated than the previous ones in that two pairs of nested oppositions are incorporated. The first is the now familiar one between the message, which he calls *meaning*, and the expression, which he calls *form*. The second is a distinction between *reduction* and *replacement* strategies.

In ordinary communication, the optimal message, conveying the optimal meaning, is the speaker's communicative goal. If the speaker has an available interlanguage form, even one obtained through formal adjustment, the conversation proceeds and the utterance is called the actual message. If the optimal meaning cannot be conveyed, then the speaker 'adjusts his meaning so as to bring it within the sphere of his encoding capabilities'. The expressed outcome of this adjustment is the adjusted meaning.

Adjusted meanings are derived in two ways. The first is to sacrifice part of the original meaning, to say less than was intended. Thus, qualifiers, relative clauses, and subsidiary information can be deleted with little damage to the essential message. This is called *meaning reduction*, and corresponds to Corder's strategy of message reduction, the least-deforming of the message adjustment strategies. The second is to substitute the message or parts of the message for alternatives which are capable of being expressed. In this way, the entire communicative goal of the speaker can be sacrificed and replaced by a new goal if the resources for achieving the original one could not be recruited. This is called *meaning replacement*. Although Varadi does not explicitly address this issue, it is plausible that one sort of replacement is a null message, leaving the speaker to give up entirely on expressing that meaning. This strategy corresponds to Corder's first three strategies, namely, topic avoidance, message abandonment, and semantic avoidance.

The second level of decision concerns manipulations to the form. These manipulations are intricately connected to the message adjustments in that they constrain the choices made for meanings to be expressed. Formal reduction involves the elimination of certain formal properties of the speaker's inter-language system, words, phrases, structures, and the like. In this way, the learner operates from a reduced system (cf. Faerch and Kasper, 1983a, described above). Formal replacement strategies are those in which alternative forms of expression are sought to achieve the established goal. In these cases, an alternative form, word, phrase, structure, is substituted for the usual target language form but the meaning remains intact. Thus, synonyms are substituted, and lengthy descriptions are generated to convey the optimal meaning. These are the strategies discussed in most taxonomies.

The pivotal point of this system, then, is message adjustment. Once a speaker decides that the optimal message cannot be expressed, the speaker must then decide whether that meaning will be reduced or replaced by an adjusted meaning; when a meaning, either optimal or adjusted, cannot be directly expressed, the speaker must then decide whether expression of that message will be based on reduction or replacement of the usual forms.

Synthesis of the Approaches

The conception of language production as the speaker's attempt to match linguistic resources to intended meaning goals is a fruitful way of classifying communication strategies. Strategies can be shown to apply primarily to one or the other of these constituents: the intended message or the preferred form of expression. The choice between these strategic options would presumably occur in the planning phase of the Faerch and Kasper model. While it is uncertain whether the generation of such strategic plans can be profitably discussed in the absence of the execution of those plans, as is the case in their model, their framework does provide an effective means for placing decisions of this sort into a larger context of language production.

In spite of the apparent consistency in the basis for classification across systems, namely, whether it is the meaning or the form that becomes modified, there is surprisingly little agreement on how the classifying dimension should be applied. This can be illustrated by examining the three systems in a single framework, as shown in table 2.4. Although the same terms recur throughout the systems, they are assigned different meanings. Thus, reduction is a

Table 2.4 Comparison of classification systems

Classification system	Strategies to manipulate meaning goal	Strategies to manipulate form
Corder	*message adjustment* increase adjustment — topic avoidance / topic abandonment / semantic avoidance / message reduction	*resource expansion* increase risk — switching / borrowing/inventing / paraphrasing / paralinguistic strategies
Faerch and Kasper	*reduction strategies* *functional* reduce intended meaning *formal* reduce system	*achievement strategies* **code switching** **interlingual transfer** **inter/intra transfer** **interlanguage-based strategies** **co-operative strategies** **nonlinguistic strategies**
Varadi	*optimal – adjusted meaning* *reduction* reduce intended meaning *replacement* change optimal meaning	*adjusted form* *reduction* reduce *replacement* paraphrasing circumlocution

popular way to describe adjustment made to optimal forms of expression, but it is used sometimes as a classification of strategies, as by Faerch and Kasper, and sometimes as a means of contrasting strategies within a classification, as by Varadi. Reduction is usually applied to the manipulation of meaning. Although Corder does not explicitly describe manipulations such as reduction, he does describe the manipulation of the form of expression as expansion, implying that the contrasting set is therefore reduction.

Second, within each classification system, one of the lists of strategies corresponds to those communication strategies most vigorously investigated in the empirical literature. These have been indicated by bold type on the table. It is significant that in all cases this fundamental set of strategies is an aspect of attempts to adjust the form of expression, and not a reflection of the attempts to adjust the meaning. This bias reflects the predominant focus of research attention on the formal or surface structure forms that are adopted in the expression of given meanings.

In sum, communication strategies overcome obstacles to communication by providing the speaker with an alternative form of expression for the intended meaning. In the process of creating these strategies, considerable compromise to the meaning initially intended may occur. Most descriptions of the changes inflicted on meaning document the extent to which portions of the ideal message have had to be avoided, deleted, or altered.

There is a danger of circularity in this analysis. The underlying assumption is that manipulation of meaning and manipulation of form are distinct options available to the speaker. Yet study of the language actually produced by speakers can in fact give direct evidence for only one of these choices, namely, manipulation of form. How are we to judge the extent to which speakers amend their original intention to bring those meanings into line with their linguistic abilities? Laboratory experiments, which will be discussed in chapters 3, 4, and 6, provide some control over the speaker's intentions and hence allow considerable inference to be made concerning adjustments to those intentions. But in general inferences of this type are not possible. The analysis of strategies based on the manipulation of meanings is mediated by the study of the manipulations of forms used by speakers. It is not surprising, then, that it is formal manipulation that appears to be primary in these classifications. That is not to say that manipulation of meaning strategies is less central; it means only that it is less observable.

To summarize, the purpose of this chapter has been to determine the boundaries for the phenomenon known as *communication strategies* and to distinguish this construct from other related phenomena. The structure of the inquiry was to begin at the broadest level and gradually narrow the focus until different types of communication strategies were being considered. Accordingly, strategies were first distinguished from processes; second, communication strategies were distinguished from learning strategies; and finally, communication strategies aimed at modifying the intended message were distinguished from those aimed at manipulating the linguistic resources. This process of narrowing and refining will be continued into the next chapter, where different ways in which the message or the linguistic resources may be manipulated will be considered.

The success of this attempted delineation may seem at this stage to be at best ambivalent. Indeed, no single criterion has been cited as irrevocably critical to the identification of a communication strategy, and no strategy has been identified as the consummate example. There are two possible explanations for this absence of clear and precise defining features. The first is that the domain of communication strategies is elusive. No formal criteria exist for the identification of this domain, and no example unequivocally illustrates the use of the domain. A strong version of this possibility is the claim that no such domain exists but that the notion of communication strategy is epiphenomenal and as such can be wholly explained through some other construct.

The second possibility is that the attempts at delineating communication strategies have been grounded in the wrong distinctions. In this view, a valid description of communication strategies simply awaits the correct approach to the problem. The descriptions discussed in the present chapter have been primarily based on theoretical argument; the descriptions presented in the next chapter are based more on empirical evidence. A different approach to a theoretical argument which can signify the role of strategies in communication will be discussed in chapter 7.

3 Taxonomies of Communication Strategies

The majority of the descriptions of communication strategies are presented as taxonomies. Taxonomies, or typologies, are systematic organizing structures for a range of events within a domain. This chapter will begin with a brief description of taxonomies and their use. The second section contains a description of the major taxonomies that have been proposed for communication strategies. The third section offers an overview of some factors that may relate to the way in which learners select a specific strategy from the taxonomy.

Organizing Structures for Science

According to Mandler (1984), the common organizing structures used in science derive from Aristotle's two associative principles. These organizing principles serve both to structure our knowledge of a domain and to delimit the logical relations that may hold among the components of knowledge. The first of Aristotle's principles is spatial/temporal contiguity, leading to *schematic structure*; the second is the principle of similarity, leading to *categorical taxonomic structures*.

Schematic structure is the basis for much of our knowledge of events, what Tulving (1972) refers to as 'episodic memory'. We have a 'scheme' for going to a fast-food outlet such as McDonalds, for example, which includes waiting in a line behind a cashier, ordering a hamburger and french fries from an illuminated menu on the back wall, taking the plastic tray to the plastic table, etc. This organization is structured around temporally contiguous events. Schemes of this type are central to such verbal activities as story comprehension (e.g. Mandler, 1984), where we fit new information from the text into pre-existing conceptual structures that determine our expectations.

The taxonomy, the second structure, is a central organizing principle in science and philosophy. Properties of similarity are extracted from a set to become the basis of grouping items or events into categories. Semantic memory is organized in this way: we associate apples and pears because they are fruits, trains and boats because they are vehicles, plumbers and carpenters because they are construction workers. Evidence for this organization is available from psycholinguistic experiments in which subjects are asked to make judgements about the similarity of two things (e.g. robin, sparrow) or the truth of a statement (e.g. 'A robin is a bird'). The time taken to respond to such items is measured in milliseconds, and shorter times are interpreted as evidence that the two events are represented as being 'closer' in semantic space. The structure for these semantic spaces is usually modelled as a taxonomy (for example, early research by Collins and Quillian, 1969; Smith et al., 1974; and review in Clark and Clark, 1977).

Taxonomic structures are highly flexible − most things can be classified in many ways. The taxonomic position of an item changes when a new feature is selected as the basis of similarity. Consider a taxonomy developed to organize *animals*. If the organizing feature is *domesticity*, then cats, dogs, goldfish, and hamsters are assigned to the same category. If *skin covering* is chosen, then the goldfish must part company with the rest. Using *ferocity* as the organizing feature, lions and vultures may be assigned to a single category in spite of different classifications regarding mobility, habitat, reproductive system, vertebrae structure, and the like. As illustrated by this example, taxonomic structures lack principled relations among members of a class, claiming only that these members share some feature. Vertical relations, however, such as those that order sets and subsets, are easily conveyed through taxonomies. Thus, living things can be classified as plants or animals, animals can be classified as vertebrates or invertebrates, vertebrates can be classified as mammals or reptiles, and so on.

There are two implications of these features of taxonomies for their use in organizing communication strategies. First, since taxonomies are simply classifications, no assumptions can be made about the internal organization or priority of the strategies within a class. If strategy A and strategy B are assigned to the same taxonomic class, one may not infer that strategy A is better or preferable to strategy B, only that the two strategies share a feature.

Second, since the structure of the taxonomy is based on an organizing feature selected by the researcher, it must be acknowledged that the strategies could change their assigned position if another feature were selected. Hence, it may not be assumed that the proposed categorical structure is in any sense 'in the head'. A different organizing principle could conceivably restructure the groupings. Because of their inherent organizational properties, taxonomies are a productive first approach to investigating a new domain. The structures that emerge from such exercises allow the researcher to pursue more rigorous theoretical and empirical examination of that domain.

Taxonomies of Strategies

Tarone's Typology

One of the earliest typologies that assembled communication strategies in an organized fashion was that of Tarone (1977). The scheme was built out of earlier work on interlanguage production (Tarone et al., 1976) but was specially tailored to model the empirical observations of a study of second-language learners' communication strategies.

The original study included nine subjects from three different language backgrounds, who were at an intermediate (but undefined) level of proficiency. These subjects were each shown two simple drawings and a complex illustration and asked to describe all three in both their native language and English. Several of the objects in the complex picture were designated as target items, and it was the attempt to convey the names of those objects that comprised the data. Thus it was possible to compare the approaches of different learners for their solution to specific communication problems. This methodology was an important contribution to the field and modifications of it have provided the basis for most of the research subsequently conducted in this area.

The data set for this seminal study was small – only nine subjects and seven target language concepts – but the scope was sufficient to uncover most of the communication strategies discussed in future studies, and at the same time show the consistency with which learners adopt these strategies in communicative situations of this type. Because Tarone's typology is typical of those that followed, and because her definitions are explicit and her examples illustrative, her categories will be examined in detail, using examples from her original study. The taxonomy is reported in table 3.1.

Table 3.1 Typology of Tarone's conscious communication strategies

1 Avoidance
a Topic avoidance
b Message abandonment
2 Paraphrase
a Approximation
b Word coinage
c Circumlocution
3 Conscious transfer
a Literal translation
b Language switch
4 Appeal for assistance
5 Mime

Source: E. Tarone, Conscious communication strategies in interlanguage: a progress report, p. 197. In *On TESOL '77*. Copyright TESOL 1977. Reprinted by permission.

The taxonomy is presented in five major categories, or strategies, with subcategories for three of them. The five major categories each reflect a different sort of decision about how to solve the communication problem.

Avoidance   Learners sometimes make a deliberate decision not to speak because they expect communication problems to arise. This avoidance is a common strategy for second-language learners, causing them to remain silent when they would otherwise contribute to a conversation simply because some aspect of vocabulary or grammar is not known. Although normally difficult to detect, Tarone's methodology made it clear when a subject was deliberately using an avoidance strategy. Omitting salient but lexically difficult objects shown in the picture, such as *mushroom* or *waterpipe*,[1] was interpreted as evidence of this strategy. Such interpretations were especially well-grounded since each subject also provided descriptions in their native language. Content discrepancies between the two data sets pointed to cases of avoidance.

Tarone refines this strategy by distinguishing between *topic avoidance* and *message abandonment*. For the former, specific topics or words are avoided to the best of the learner's ability. Learners, that is, manage to prevent the occurrence of topics that are certain to present difficulties. For the latter, learners stumble into a topic that is too difficult and simply give up and go on to another. In this case, one might say that the learner should have avoided the topic altogether since no real effort was made to conquer the problem.

Avoidance, then, is one way to assure that communication continues. It is a slippery strategy from the point of view of both the learner and the researcher. For the learner, restricting conversation to those topics that are well controlled linguistically is arguably an ineffective way to communicate or to improve competence with the language. For the researcher, it is sometimes a value judgement to claim that a learner has avoided a topic as opposed to simply chosen not to discuss it, as we would claim of a native speaker. Even message abandonment can indicate a change of intention and not a fear of linguistic challenge.

Paraphrase   Tarone defines paraphrase as 'the rewording of the message in an alternate, acceptable target language construction, in situations where the appropriate form or construction is not known or not yet stable' (p. 198). This is a broad category and within it, Tarone identifies three types of paraphrase strategies. The first is *approximation*, which she defines as 'the use of a single target language vocabulary item or structure, which the learner knows is not correct, but which shares enough semantic features in common with the desired item to satisfy the learner' (p. 198). Approximation, then, includes virtually all word substitutions that the learner knowingly employs to serve in place of the more accurate term. The substitute word can refer to the correct concept but at an inappropriate level, such as *worm* for *silkworm*, or refer to another object that may give some hint to the intended referent, such as *lamp* for *waterpipe*.

The second paraphrase strategy is *word coinage*, 'the learner makes up a new word in order to communicate a desired concept' (p. 198). The most frequently cited example of this strategy is one originally reported by Varadi (1973) in which *airball* was created to refer to *balloon*. Tarone provides the example of one subject who used *person worm* to refer to a picture of an animated caterpillar. This example is somewhat confusing, however, since the intended concept does not have a clear appropriate label, and the product of the strategy is itself not a single invented word. In our own research studying English-speaking learners of French (Bialystok and Frohlich, 1980), one subject created *heurot* to mean *clock*. The strategy was to base the word *clock* on the French word *heure*. In general, clear cases of word coinage are less common than are instances of the other types of paraphrase strategies.

The final paraphrase strategy, *circumlocution*, 'is a wordly [*sic*] extended process in which the learner describes the characteristics or elements of the object or action instead of using the appropriate target language structure' (p. 198). The example Tarone gives from her study is a subject attempting to refer to waterpipe: 'She is, uh, smoking something. I don't know what's its name. That's uh, Persian, and we use in Turkey, a lot of.' Here the learner is groping for features that may help the listener guess what the intended object might be. Most examples in the literature, however, are far more explicit in isolating features that are highly indicative of the object and putting them into a description. In our study of French learners, the following circumlocutions were provided for *tabouret* (bench): *une petite chaise de bois* (a little wooden chair), *pour reposer les jambes quand on est fatigué* (to rest your legs when you are tired), *elle n'a pas de dos* (it doesn't have a back).

Tarone's terminological use of paraphrase as the major strategy and circumlocution as a subtype is not typical of their use in most other taxonomies where paraphrase and circumlocution are assigned more equivalent status. Blum-Kulka and Levenston (1983) point out that the use of these terms in translation is quite different. In that domain, circumlocutions provide all relevant semantic features for an item, while paraphrase is a last resort that points to only a rough equivalent. On this definition, paraphrase would not be assigned superordinate status.

Conscious Transfer   Conscious transfer has two manifestations. The first is in the literal translation of words or phrases, and the second in the interspersals of words from another language. Her example of *literal translation* is a Mandarin speaker who translated the Mandarin toast and produced 'He invites him to drink'. *Language switch* is the straightforward insertion of words from another language. In an extension of this work, Tarone (1981) changed the name of this strategy to *borrowing* but kept the two subtypes of literal translation and language switch.

Appeal for Assistance   An appeal for assistance has occurred when the learner has consulted any source of authority: a native speaker, the experimenter, a dictionary. The strategy is often smuggled into other more verbal efforts, however, by such prosodic features as rising intonation which implicitly elicits some assistance or validation from the listener.

Mime   This final strategy includes all nonverbal accompaniments to communication, particularly those that serve in the place of a missing target-language word. Some concepts are easy to simulate, such as Tarone's example of the subject clapping his hands to indicate applause, but other gestures are considerably less interpretable by a listener.

Later Taxonomies

An important contribution to the classification of communication strategies was made by Varadi (1980). Although his study did not appear until after the publication of Tarone's taxonomy, it is clear that an earlier version of his work which was given as a conference paper in 1973 (and was not widely available) was influential in the development of Tarone's ideas.

Varadi's work is based on the premise that communication strategies involve various kinds of *message adjustment*. He distinguishes between adjustment that is attributed to *reduction* and that which is attributed to *replacement*. At the same time he differentiates *intensional* from *extensional* reduction. These varieties of reduction converge on the strategies of generalization and approximation, respectively. In all these cases of reduction, an imprecise term lacking in some specific features is substituted for the intended concept. He gives the examples of substituting *ball* for *balloon*, or *rope* for *clothes-line* to illustrate generalization, and *gas ball*, or *air ball* for *balloon* and *string* for *clothes-line* to illustrate approximation. The intended difference between generalization and approximation, however, is not clear from these examples.

Replacement strategies include circumlocution and paraphrase, familiar from Tarone's taxonomy. Circumlocution is illustrated by *special toys for children*, and paraphrase by *they are filled by gas* for *balloon*. Again, the examples do not clearly demarcate the critical differences between these strategies.

The taxonomy is more restricted than Tarone's, presumably because Varadi was interested only in describing categories of message adjustment. All his strategies, in fact, belong to the category of paraphrase in Tarone's system.

Other taxonomies have been proposed, the differences between them being the general categories proposed and demarcation of specific examples of those strategies. In our own work, for example (Bialystok and Frohlich, 1980; Bialystok, 1983), the taxonomy is organized around the source of information that is the basis of the strategy. Accordingly, the taxonomy is structured around the three categories of *L1-based strategies*, *L2-based strategies*, and *paralinguistic strategies*. There are three types of L1-based strategies: *language switch*, which is the insertion of a word or phrase from another language; *foreignizing*, in which some target-language modification is applied to the L1 term (for example, pronouncing the English *pressure* with a French accent to create a possible French word for 'pressure' instead of the correct *pression*); and *transliteration*, in which some literal translation of a phrase is used (for example, using *place de feu* to convey the English *fireplace*). Language switch and literal translation correspond directly to Tarone's two forms of conscious transfer while foreignizing adds a further distinction. There are three types of L2-based strategies: *semantic contiguity*, which corresponds to Tarone's approximation; *description*, further explicated into a number of substrategies and corresponding to *circumlocution*; and *word coinage*, much as described by Tarone.

Although the strategies identified in this taxonomy are similar to those appearing in Tarone's, their organization is different. The intention in this classification is to identify the source of information that the learner has drawn upon to solve the communication problem. Following Corder (1983), the principle of this taxonomy is that communication can be achieved by following various routes to meaning, and strategies provide alternative routes.

Another organizational principle is suggested by Faerch and Kasper (1983a). They categorize communication strategies in terms of the learner's attempt to *avoid* the difficulty, thereby choosing a *reduction strategy*, or to *achieve* some solution, thereby selecting an *achievement strategy*. Their taxonomy was presented in table 2.4. The central claim is that the outcome of using each of these categories of communication strategies is different. If the learner's behaviour is motivated by avoidance and a reduction strategy is chosen, then the result is that the learner changes or modifies the original communicative goal. If the learner's behaviour is motivated by achievement and an achievement strategy is chosen, then the result is that the learner changes the plans to realize the communicative goal, leaving the original goal intact. Thus the two categories of strategies operate by altering different aspects of the language production process (at least as that process is described by Faerch and Kasper).

Faerch and Kasper further distinguish between *formal reduction*, in which parts of the linguistic system are avoided, and *functional reduction*, in which the speaker's communicative intentions are abandoned or reduced. There is, however, an inextricable link between these two, blurring considerably the intended distinction. If one engages in *lexical formal reduction*, for example, because the speaker cannot cope with the target-language word for *mushroom*, one necessarily engages in *functional reduction* by avoiding all discussion pertaining to edible fungi. In short, it is not clear in what sense these are separate events.

The list of strategies that comprise the *reduction strategies* corresponds roughly to Tarone's avoidance strategy. Faerch and Kasper make some finer distinctions, proposing topic avoidance, message abandonment, and meaning replacement. They admit the boundaries between these strategies are fuzzy so suggest that they be considered as points along a continuum: 'At the one end, the learner says "almost" what he wants to say about a given topic (= meaning replacement), at the other end he says nothing at all about this (= topic avoidance)' (p. 44).

The achievement strategies are also further subdivided by Faerch and Kasper. One type, *retrieval strategies*, refers to the attempts made by the learner to retrieve, or remember, the optimal form. They identify the following six retrieval strategies: waiting for the term to appear; appealing to formal similarity; retrieval via semantic fields; searching via other languages; retrieval from learning situations; sensory procedures. These activities appear to be of a different order to those normally included in the taxonomy of communication strategies. Most classification systems are based on the assumption that the learner has already attempted a thorough search of available knowledge in order to recall the required form and is truly experiencing a gap. We assume, that is, that learners prefer to use the optimal form, if only they can remember it!

The second type, *compensatory strategies*, includes the usual techniques that have become familiar in the taxonomies but introduce some further distinctions. The strategies they propose are: code switching; interlingual transfer (from any other language); inter-/intralingual transfer (overgeneralization of L2 forms based on L1 structures); interlanguage-based strategies (including the familiar (i) generalization, cf. Tarone's approximation, (ii) paraphrase, cf. Tarone's circumlocution, (iii) word coinage, and (iv) restructuring). Restructuring is reminiscent of Tarone's message abandonment and they define it as follows: 'a restructuring strategy is used whenever the learner realizes that he cannot complete a local plan which he has already begun realizing and develops an alternative local plan which enables him to communicate his intended message without reduction' (p. 50). They provide the following example: 'my tummy – my tummy is – I have [inaudible] I must eat something' (p. 50). In other words, the learner changes his mind halfway through the utterance. One can only wonder at what point the change in intention would be classified as topic avoidance or formal lexical reduction and not a restructuring compensatory strategy. Finally, they also include co-operative strategies, which are essentially versions of Tarone's appeal for assistance, and nonlinguistic strategies, capturing Tarone's mime.

Faerch and Kasper's taxonomy is more complex than the others, containing both more distinctions and more subtypes. The organizing basis for the major categorization in the taxonomy is the learner's intention either to avoid the problem or to achieve some solution to it. This intentional basis is inferred from the linguistic data: speakers who give up on a topic are assumed to be motivated by avoidance, while those who embark upon loquacious explanation are assumed to be motivated by success. Within the subtype compensatory strategy, the list of six exemplifying strategies is highly convergent with the five major strategies proposed by Tarone. The additional category inserted by Faerch and Kasper is inter-/intralingual transfer, but this strategy appears to be a variation of Tarone's conscious transfer or Bialystok's foreignizing.

The final taxonomy to be examined is that developed by Paribakht (1985). She proposes that there are four possible approaches to the communication problem: linguistic approach; contextual approach; conceptual approach; and mime. These approaches are distinguished by their reliance on different types of knowledge that become incorporated into the strategy. The linguistic approach exploits semantic features of the referent object, the contextual approach exploits contextual knowledge surrounding the referent object, the conceptual approach exploits the speaker's general knowledge of the world, and mime exploits knowledge of meaningful gestures. The first three approaches are more or less scaled along a continuum or generality, the sources of knowledge increasingly widening out from the specific properties of the object to a larger contextual context. Mime is discontinuous with this scale because no specification concerning the nature of the information incorporated into those 'meaningful gestures' is made. A summary of Paribakht's taxonomy is presented in table 3.2.

The proliferation of general categories is an attempt to be more precise about identifying the source of information recruited to solve the communication problem. Each of these is presumably involved in communication. In these terms, the function of a communication strategy is to deliberately call upon one of them to compensate for linguistic gaps. The use of these four approaches in organizing strategies, however, produces a fairly uneven taxonomy. Most of the strategies familiar from the other systems are considered here as part of the linguistic approach. These include the strategies of *circumlocution*, various kinds of *description*, and some more specific versions of these called *comparison*. The contextual and conceptual approaches are attempts to account for related information that the speaker provides about the intended concept. Much of the information incorporated into these strategies is specific to items and to cultures. An attempt to explain *lantern*, for example, produced, 'You may use it in camping'. Although that would probably be classified as something like *circumlocution* or *description of function* in most of the shorter taxonomies, it is used here as an instance of *exemplification*, part of the conceptual approach. Similarly, Persian-speaking subjects provided the following utterance to explain *fate*. 'Some say, it's written on your forehead.' This is a transliteration of a Persian idiom, interpretable only to other Persian-speakers, and is classified as the contextual approach. The elaboration of alternatives in this taxonomy, then, captures differences in background knowledge and use of information to convey target concepts. At issue, however, is the extent to which this larger repertoire also reflects an increase in the number of strategic choices available to speakers.

Summary of the Taxonomies

The sample of taxonomies described here provides an overview of the systems that have been proposed. Each is organized around a different criterion, yet the similarity in the strategies listed, and, to some extent, even in their classification, is striking. The criteria for choosing a solution type, being motivated to reduce or achieve, or consulting different sources of information from the mental repertoire led to similar classifications of the utterances produced by different learners, having different language backgrounds, and

Table 3.2 Summary of Paribakht's taxonomy

I **Linguistic approach**
  A Semantic continuity
    1 Superordinate
    2 Comparison
      a Positive comparison
        i Analogy
        ii Synonymy
      b Negative comparison
        i Contrast and opposition
        ii Antonymy
  B Circumlocution
    1 Physical description
      a Size
      b Shape
      c Colour
      d Material
    2 Constituent features
      a Features
      b Elaborated features
    3 Locational property
    4 Historical property
    5 Other features
    6 Functional description
  C Metalinguistic clues

II **Contextual approach**
  A Linguistic context
  B Use of TL idioms and proverbs
  C Transliteration of L1 idioms and proverbs
  D Idiomatic transfer

III **Conceptual approach**
  A Demonstration
  B Exemplification
  C Metonymy

IV **Mime**
  A Replacing verbal output
  B Accompanying verbal output

Source: T. Paribakht, Strategic competence and language proficiency. *Applied Linguistics*, 6, 132–46, 1985. Reprinted by permission.

solving different communication problems. At the core of communication strategies, then, is a real phenomenon that is in need of explanation. What language or communication processes are responsible for learner's behaviour in these situations such that a common set of linguistic patterns is reliably demonstrated under conditions of such diversity?

There are, of course, possible explanations for this convergence that have little to do with communication or language processing. Researchers build on the work of their colleagues by taking existing suggestions for taxonomic distinctions as a starting-point and refining them to fit their own ideas. It is not surprising, then, to find continuity in the analysis of a problem.

Another possibility is that the differences between the chosen criteria are apparent and not real. The organization of the taxonomies in this case would simply be different surface structure reflections of the same underlying structure. All the criteria for organizing the taxonomies, that is, would be different expressions of the same critical communicative difference. It is plausible that the decision to describe a concept (Tarone's *paraphrase*) necessarily implicates extended use of the target language (L2-based strategy for Bialystok, and Faerch and Kasper), all of which is indispensably motivated by achievement (Faerch and Kasper's achievement strategy). To return to zoological taxonomies, classifying animals according to either their ability to fly or their possession of feathers will lead to essentially the same typology. In this way, a set of converging descriptions will lead to the same classification of events, even though the criteria for classifying the events appear to be different.

The research addressing the identification of communication strategies has reached a general consensus about what constitutes the range of behaviours exhibited by second-language learners under conditions of potential communication collapse. This consensus is particularly significant in that, unlike scientific classifications, the development of these taxonomies involves two distinct steps. If one is asked to produce a classification system for animals, for example, one simply lists all the animals relevant to the problem then proceeds to categorize them by extracting some relevant criterion and assigning animals to groups according to this. The task is more complex for communication strategies because it is impossible at the outset to list the relevant strategies. These must be wrested from the transcripts of speech produced by speakers in a variety of communicative exchanges. Classification of these strategies can only proceed once they have been discovered. It is notable, then, that the agreement among the researchers extends to both the identification of the relevant strategies and to their categorization.

Finally, it is important to emphasize that all the taxonomies are descriptions of linguistic utterances but are addressed to the problem of learner behaviour. On the basis of the form of language produced, the claim is that the learner has used a particular strategy. The organization of utterances in the taxonomies is based on various levels of inference concerning the underlying mental processes, or behaviour, that produced them. Tarone is most neutral on the process issue, claiming only that the language used to solve a problem indicates certain options that could have been followed. Faerch and Kasper are most 'mentalistic', claiming that strategy choices are associated with certain mental dispositions or orientations. But such claims remain inferential. The fact that the communication strategies can be organized in a certain way does not in any sense imply that such organization also exists as a mental structure for the language learner. Taxonomies, that is, are not necessarily 'in the head'.

Accordingly, it remains an empirical question to determine the extent to which such strategies are organized in this way for learners (if in fact they are organized at all), and the extent to which learners are even aware of the set of strategic options and the choices they make. Tarone pursued the issue of consciousness by interviewing her subjects after the experiment to explore their reflections on the problems they were experiencing and the choices they made. The results of these interviews, however, are not reported. In any event, subjects' *post hoc* reflections on their own performance are notoriously inaccurate. The issues of the organization of these strategies for the learner and the learner's consciousness of the strategies and their organization must be explored empirically.

Factors in the Selection of Strategies

One way of establishing whether or not the communication strategies are an organized set of options for language learners is to determine whether the selection of specific strategies is governed by identifiable factors. If the selection of the specific categories that organize the taxonomies could be predicted by reliable factors, then the organization of those taxonomies would be validated. Potential factors in this regard are the proficiency of the learner, features of the communicative situation, and the nature of the task. If there were no relation between such factors and the choice of specific strategies, then there would be no evidence to substantiate the claim that the communication strategies are represented for learners as an organized set of options. Random selection of strategies, at least concerning these situational factors, would indicate either that the strategies are selected on an *ad hoc* basis, or that the actual organizing principle is not captured in the taxonomies. Are there, then, predictable ways in which learners select strategies?

Proficiency of the Learner

The first factor that may be expected to predict the choice of a specific communication strategy is the proficiency level of the speaker. The strategies make different linguistic demands, and some may be too sophisticated for less advanced language learners. Some studies have attempted to look at the relation between L2 proficiency and strategy choice, but results are either mixed or inconclusive.

Tarone attempted an informal examination of this question. She rank-ordered her subjects 'in what I *estimated* [emphasis added] to be a rough order of proficiency to [*sic*] English' (1977, p. 202) and tabulated the number of times they used each strategy. The resulting distribution showed different selection patterns for each of the nine subjects (although paraphrase was usually the preferred strategy). Tarone acknowledges that personality differences among the subjects may account for these patterns, but claims as well 'that strategy preference and second-language proficiency level may prove to be related' (p. 202). Although the hypothesis is worth pursuing, support for it is absent in her data.

Other studies have been more explicit in testing the hypothesis that there is a relation between proficiency and strategy selection. In one study, we examined the use of communication strategies by 17-year-old students in a French as a second language class (Bialystok, 1983). The students were taken from either an advanced or a regular class, and their grades, test scores, and pretest results (all students were administered a cloze test to assess their proficiency in French) confirmed the designation as advanced or regular. The results showed that the advanced students used proportionally more L2-based strategies than did the regular students, who relied more on the L1-based strategies. But does this mean that advanced learners select strategies differently? A group of adult learners of French, who were more advanced than any of the students, showed overall selection patterns similar to those of the regular students. On average, then, these advanced learners did not shun the L1-based strategies in the same way as did the advanced student learners.

A more detailed analysis of the selection patterns of individual learners showed a different effect. For the two groups of students, there was no correlation between their French achievement as measured by performance on a cloze test and their tendency to select L1- or L2-based strategies. This means that within each of these two classes, it was not necessarily the best students who used the L2-based strategies and the weaker students who used the L1-based strategies. The classes as a whole, however, differed in their reliance on each of these types. For the adults there was a negative correlation between achievement measured by cloze test scores and use of L1-based strategies. Thus, for the adults, it was the case that the more proficient speakers relied more on L2-based strategies.

The relation between proficiency and strategy selection revealed by these results is not simple. The explanation for the group differences in overall selection of L1- or L2-based strategies by the two student classes may be a tendency to compliance. Successful students are those who follow the rules in school, and one rule in The French class is not to use English. For this reason, students in the advanced class make a greater effort to avoid English. The more detailed individual analysis shows that this tendency is not related to the proficiency of the individual student. Individual analysis of adult selection patterns, however, does reveal a relation between level of proficiency and the differential selection of a broad taxonomic class of communication strategies. Hence, one cannot rule out the hypothesis that selection of strategy types is determined by the learner's proficiency level. That such a difference is evidenced in the selection of an L1- or L2-based strategy is entirely reasonable since the L2-based strategies place considerably greater demands upon the linguistic resources of the speaker. The absence of any indication of a relation at a finer level of analysis, that is, in the selection of specific strategies within these taxonomic categories, however, diminishes the interest of the obtained finding.

Other studies have also produced equivocal results. The detailed taxonomy developed by Paribakht (1985) allowed her to examine precise relations between speaker proficiency and strategy choice. In her study, native speakers of Persian, who were advanced or intermediate learners of English, and native speakers of English completed a set of communication tasks. Their strategic choices were examined in terms of the four approaches that organized her taxonomy: linguistic; contextual; conceptual; and mime. There were some differences between the groups for three of the four approaches, but no consistent pattern. The linguistic approach was used most often by the native English speakers and advanced learners. These were the two groups with the greatest linguistic resources, so were perhaps most able to use this approach. The contextual approach was used equally by all three groups. The conceptual approach was used most by the intermediate learners. This is perhaps a compensatory strategy for the lack of use of the linguistic approach (but see the discussion above about possible confounding in assigning strategies to these two approaches). Mime was used by the learners more than by the native English speakers. Again, nonstrategic reasons for this difference can be imagined. Possibly the two learners needed to compensate more for lack of linguistic resources, or possibly cultural differences made the choice of mime more natural for the learner groups.

Elicitation Task

A large number of procedures have been used to produce the data upon which analyses of communication strategies have been based. The elicitation methods include picture description (Bialystok and Frohlich, 1980; Varadi, 1980), picture reconstruction (Bialystok, 1983), translation (Galvan and Campbell, 1979; Varadi, 1980); sentence completion (Blum-Kulka and Levenston, 1983), conversation (Haastrup and Phillipson, 1983), narration (Dechert, 1983; Raupach, 1983), instruction (Wagner, 1983), word transmission (Paribakht, 1985), and interview (Raupach, 1983). These method-ological differences may influence a language learner's selection of a specific communication strategy. Returning again to the analogy with taxonomies of animals, the procedures for observing an animal's behaviour in its natural environment, in a threatening situation, under conditions of hunger/thirst, etc., would all lead to the detection of different behaviours. These different behaviours may well result in different classifications of the animals.

There are few studies that compare performance of a single subject across methods, since each researcher tends to use only one procedure. Comparisons across tasks, then, tend to be highly inferential. The problem of comparison is exacerbated by the fact that few researchers report the extent to which specific strategies were selected. Rather, categorical data indicating that a strategy was or was not used is more usually provided. Haastrup and Phillipson (1983), for example, in their analysis of communication strategies occurring in a conversation between a native speaker and a language learner, report only whether a strategy was used 'regularly' or whether a class of strategies (i.e. L1-based strategies) was used 'occasionally'. Cursory examination of these and similar results shows little systematic variation in the patterns of selection that can be attributed to the types of elicitation methods used. The more naturalistic conversation used by Haastrup and Phillipson, for example, produced about the same selection pattern as did more controlled laboratory studies: paraphrase was heavily used, some borrowing and transliteration were evident, word coinage was rare.

A more direct test of the effect of elicitation method was carried out in a study by Bialystok and Frohlich (1980). In that study, subjects were taken from a French class and randomly assigned to three groups. In one group, subjects were shown a complex picture and asked to write a description of it. The importance of being thorough and exact was stressed in the instructions. In the second group, subjects were shown the same picture but asked to describe it orally. These descriptions were recorded and later transcribed. In the third group, subjects were shown a picture and asked to describe it so that another student could recreate it on a felt board out of a group of constituent pieces that were provided. The student who was responsible for assembling the picture did not engage in any verbal interaction with the describer, but the describer was able to monitor the description by observing the emerging picture. The three methods produced quantitative differences in the amount of elicited speech, the written composition yielding the least and the reconstruction the most. However, the qualitative features of the speech in terms of the classification of strategic choices was in all cases equivalent. The students, that is, employed the same set of strategies in roughly the same proportions irrespective of the elicitation method used.

In spite of the lack of generalized effect of the elicitation method, idiosyncracies of specific tasks undoubtedly introduce some bias. Blum and Levenston (1978), for example, suggest that subjects performing their sentence-completion task were restricted to inserting single-word responses and hence biased against the use of such strategies as circumlocution. It is equally obvious that strategies such as mime and appeal for assistance are precluded by written or noninteractive tasks. The purpose is not to find what strategies are permitted by different elicitation procedures, but to determine whether identifiable patterns of selection from the permitted strategies can be traced to those procedures.

Faerch and Kasper (1983a) suggest that the choice of a strategy relates, not so much to the task, but to the nature of the problem. They claim that: 'problems that relate to fluency and correctness constitute a special class in that they frequently cause the language user not to use the most "obvious" parts of his IL system because he expects that there will be problems in realizing them' (p. 37). In these cases, learners would be biased towards reduction strategies in order to avoid using potentially problematic parts of their linguistic repertoire. No evidence for this conjecture was offered. The opposite outcome is, however, equally conceivable. If students were to perceive a problem to be a test of fluency, they would undoubtedly make different choices.

The type of elicitation method is important in determining the strategies that will be observed. It is clear that learners will adjust the way in which they approach a problem according to their perception of what is relevant. Communication with a teacher in a language classroom will lead to different uses of the language than will conversations with a friend. The problem is that the literature has not been able to document with any precision how these different kinds of situations translate into the selection of different communication strategies. Any differences that might emerge from such different contexts as speaking to a teacher and chatting with a friend may well be more a function of the different sociolinguistic settings than of any difference in choice among communication strategies.

Influence of the First Language

It is plausible to propose that second-language learners who differ in their first language select differently from the taxonomy of communication strategies. Undoubtedly the *form* of certain strategies will change as a function of the speaker's L1, particularly for such strategies as conscious transfer. But do learners from different language backgrounds *select* differently from the strategies? Tarone's study included three learners from each of three language backgrounds and found no tendencies for these language backgrounds to lead to different patterns of selection. Larger samples, however, may reveal more systematic patterns.

One area that has received much research attention recently is language transfer, referred to by Kellerman and Sharwood Smith (1986) by the more neutral term *cross-linguistic influence*. Part of this cross-linguistic influence includes the insertion of L1 terms into L2 speech, constituting the communication strategy of *conscious transfer*. Kellerman (1978, 1984) has shown how learners differentially transfer terms from an L1 to an L2 as a function of a number of factors. The first is the learner's perception of the distance between the L1 and the L2. Languages which are *perceived* to be similar (whether or not they actually are) are more likely to lead to transfer than those which are not. Other factors involve the target term, and the extent to which that term is used in a typical sense in that context. Hence, selection of the communication strategies that involve transfer, or the L1-based strategies, should be sensitive to the same constraints. More frequent use of the L1-based strategies should be evident in learners communicating in an L2 that they perceive to be related to their L1 and in contexts that satisfy the criterion of typicality. Unfortunately, the hypothesis has not been empirically tested.

Ringbom (1987) has shown how the hypotheses of linguistic similarity and the corresponding willingness to transfer from the L1 also underlies second-language learning. In his study, Swedish-speaking and Finnish-speaking learners of English who were all Finnish and learning under similar conditions differentially relied on knowledge of the L1. The Swedish-speakers were significantly more willing to transfer L1 vocabulary than were the Finnish-speakers.

Since there is no systematic study which allows for direct comparison of strategy selection by subjects who differ in their L1, one can only make broad comparisons across studies which have drawn upon subjects with different language backgrounds. Specific studies tend to base the results on language learners with the same L1 learning the same L2. Hence, Varadi (1980) studied Hungarian-speaking learners of English, Bialystok and Frohlich (1980) studied English-speaking learners of French, and Faerch and Kasper (1983a, b) studied Danish-speaking learners of English. Cursory examination of the results of these studies gives no hint that the native language of the subjects influenced the selection patterns observed. All of the studies have produced reasonably consistent patterns for the selection of communication strategies.

Speaking in a Second Language

One possibility not directly examined so far is that the relevant factor is simply that the speaker is a second-language learner. In that case, we would expect all second-language learners to behave in roughly the same way and that this would be distinct from the patterns of selection that might be observed from native speakers. Research in referential communication (e.g. Krauss and Weinheimer, 1964; Clark and Wilkes-Gibbs, 1986), discussed in chapter 5, suggests that the solutions adults adopt for problems in speaking their native language are similar to those used by second-language learners. A comparison of the solutions to communication problems adopted in a first and second language can determine the extent to which the selection of a strategy is a function of speaking in a second language.

Because of large differences in the types of task demands imposed by the research studying communication in a first language and that carried out with second-language learners, direct comparison of the strategies used and the ways in which they are selected is not really possible. A number of studies of second-language learners, however, have included native-speaker data, permitting one to examine the difference attributable to speaking in a second language *per se*. The most controlled data are those from studies in which the same learners provided descriptions in both their first and second languages.

Tarone (1977) elicited native and second-language descriptions from her subjects, but it appears from the report of her research that she referred to the native-language transcripts only casually. Her task did not allow for much analysis of the native-speaker data since all the target words would have been known to subjects and communicative problems would not have been encountered.

A more systematic attempt to compare strategies used by native speakers to those of second-language learners was evident in the study by Paribakht (1982). In her study, Persian-speaking learners of English and native English speakers participated in the same communication task. Subjects were required to convey the name of an object which was pictured on a card to a native-speaking listener. For the native speakers, the task was equally challenging since the pictured objects were unfamiliar to the English speakers, showing such objects as a *palanquin* and an *aqueduct*. Accordingly, she could compare the communication strategies selected by the two groups. The results showed few qualitative differences in the selection of the strategies (see discussion above for comparison by proficiency level). The native speakers could not, of course, use some of the more culturally based strategies described by the contextual approach, but this limitation did not translate into selection differences by the native-speaker and learner groups. In fact, contextual approach was the only one of the four to demonstrate no intergroup differences in selection.

Another attempt to compare native and non-native data was undertaken in the Nijmegen project (discussed in chapter 6). Again, subjects completing a description task in their first and second languages consistently solved the problem in the same way.

The combination of evidence from adults using communication strategies in their first language, and second-language learners repeating a particular communication task in their first language points to the conclusion that the fact of speaking a second language does not by itself determine how the communication problems will be solved. The solutions adopted for second-language communication are just as prevalent when speaking a first language.

Summary of Factors Controlling Selection

Only a small amount of research has addressed the factors that relate to the way in which learners select communication strategies. In addition to those reviewed here, a few other factors have been examined. Bialystok (1983) and Paribakht (1982) considered the effect of the target concept to determine whether different kinds of items bias learners to select different strategies. In the Bialystok study, different concrete items tended to elicit a type of description most appropriate to that item. These optimal strategies were sometimes assigned different taxonomic classification. *Tabouret* (bench), for example, was best described as 'A kind of a chair' (semantic contiguity or approximation) while *soufflet* (bellows) was best described by the action it performs, 'You use it to blow air on to a fire' (description or circumlocution). Similarly, Paribakht compared the strategies recruited to communicate concrete and abstract nouns. There were differences here too, concrete nouns taking more of the descriptive categories than did the abstract nouns. But such differences are not surprising and tell us little about the validity of the taxonomy except that it is sensitive to differences in the intended concept. The implication of this correspondence between certain concepts and certain strategy types will be explored in chapter 6.

Another possible source of systematic variance in the selection of strategies is the personality of the speaker. Tarone (1977) suggested that certain personality characteristics may be associated with preferences for avoidance strategies or appeal for assistance strategies. Beebe (1983) has examined the learner's ability to take risks as the relevant characteristic in determining the style of strategy use. These studies are so far inconclusive and further investigation is required.

In all the studies that have attempted to establish systematic links between specific factors and the selection of communication strategies, few meaningful relations have emerged. The language learners in all these studies, despite tremendous diversity, selected similarly from the range of strategies identified in the taxonomies. Some adjustments in selection were made for the concept being expressed, and more advanced learners were more confident with L2-based strategies. But essentially no single factor emerged which served to skew the selection distribution in such as way that it could be claimed that the selection of a specific communication strategy could be predicted by the presence of that factor.

What, then, is the status of the taxonomic descriptions of communication strategies? In this chapter a number of taxonomies have been reviewed and some hypotheses about what factors might influence the selection of specific strategies have been explored. The taxonomies appear on the surface to be highly contradictory, employing different degrees of refinement, using terms in different ways, and making different assumptions about how they relate to the learner's linguistic system. None the less, they demonstrate an overriding commonality. At the same time, the factors examined for their controlling role in the selection of specific strategies reveal relations that are either so obvious as to be trivial or fail to explain variation in strategy selection.

The validity of a construct is determined by the extent to which the measure of the construct reflects an actual phenomenon. IQ tests, for example, are very reliable in that people consistently obtain similar scores on subsequent retests, scores are internally consistent on a single test, and different test administrations (different examiner, different scorer, etc.) make little difference to test results. But the validity of IQ test scores is dubious. Does the score reflect some real aspect of human intelligence? Validity is the extent to which a score or description is a measure of what it is claimed to be, and on this point IQ tests have been severely challenged (see Gould, 1981, for an excellent discussion of this issue).

The taxonomies reviewed in this chapter are descriptions of the way in which second-language learners solve communication problems. The taxonomies have been extremely useful in identifying and organizing the range of behaviours that need to be considered in an explanation of communication strategies. Different researchers using different methodologies and studying different kinds of subjects have more or less agreed on the sorts of things that second-language learners do in order to communicate. In this way, at least, the taxonomies have succeeded where attempts at definition have floundered. It is clear from the taxonomies what phenomenon is in need of explanation.

If the taxonomic descriptions are valid, then the distinctions should correspond to real alternatives or real choices experienced (at some level although not necessarily consciously) by the learner. To this end, the distinctions should be apparent through behaviour, and the conditions for selecting a different strategy should be identifiable. If the communication strategies documented in all the taxonomies and presented in the literature as the repertoire of options for second-language learners is to be proven valid, then some evidence for their systematic use by learners is needed. Yet the examination thus far has shown that the events usually considered as the communication strategies used by second-language learners are based on surface linguistic variations and are not predictable from situational constraints, such as proficiency, language, and the like. These issues of the reliability and the validity of the taxonomic classifications will be examined more carefully in the next chapter.

4 Empirical Evaluation of the Taxonomies

The purpose of this chapter is to examine the extent to which the taxonomic classifications of communication strategies described in chapter 3 correspond to the types of decisions made by speakers and listeners using these strategies. This examination will be based on data from an empirical study of young second-language learners.

In chapter 3 it was shown that the taxonomies capture important features of the referential speech of second-language learners. Moreover, the classification system developed by Tarone has proven robust and complete − subsequent taxonomies can invariably be traced to her original categories, and data collected by different researchers for different purposes has confirmed the logic and utility of her distinctions. But the interpretations of those behaviours has always been confined to linguistic description. The taxonomies, that is, document the linguistic variations that signal the existence of some communication strategy. The next problem is to examine the way learners use these communication strategies and search for explanation: what is the conceptual status of communication strategies? What are the processing options that determine distinctions among strategies?

The question pursued in this chapter is the extent to which the taxonomic distinctions provide the basis for explanations of communicative behaviour in language production. Ultimately the goal of this analysis is to explain communication strategies within some more general view of language processing.

In order for communication strategies to be integrated into the mechanisms and processes of language processing, then the distinctions among the strategies must signal or reflect differences in language processing. From the point of view of processing, that is, differences between strategies are warranted if and only if they correspond to differences in processing. This is a common form of argument in psycholinguistics. Phonemes, for example, are identified by virtue of corresponding to changes in meaning, and their existence is validated because a change in phoneme reliably predicts a meaning change. Similarly, strategies must be distinguished by virtue of corresponding to some consequence on language comprehension or production.

The obvious place to begin the search for these distinctions among communication strategies that reflect differences in language processing is the linguistic taxonomies. Accordingly, the strategies identified in the taxonomies will be examined for their applicability to an explanation of the communicative behaviour of second-language learners.

In order to serve as explanations of communicative behaviour, the taxonomies must be shown to provide reliable and valid descriptions of the choices made by second-language learners. *Reliability* is determined by replicability − would different raters classify utterances in the same way? Would the same rater classify an utterance the same way on different occasions? Is the pattern of selection that emerges for a learner (or group of learners) replicable? *Validity* is determined by authenticity − do the strategies listed in the taxonomies correspond in a real sense to what learners are doing? Do the distinctions identified in the taxonomies reflect real differences in these strategies?

The potential of the taxonomies for describing learners' behaviour (as opposed to learners' utterances) will be considered by means of data from an empirical study.[1] The study is an examination of the communication strategies of a group of 9-year-old English-speaking children learning French in immersion programmes. To address issues of reliability, the utterances collected in this corpus were classified in a standard taxonomy. The validity was addressed by seeking relations between the use of specific strategic options and different communicative outcomes. The results of this study will be used to reassess the use of descriptive taxonomies with the aim of establishing a new basis for the analysis of second-language communication strategies.

Evaluation of Taxonomic Distinctions

The purpose of this study was to test the reliability and validity of the taxonomic descriptions of communication strategies. The data consisted of the strategies chosen by second-language learners to solve a communication problem and the effects of those choices on listeners' comprehension. The design allowed for the data to be classified according to different descriptive systems and for the effects of the strategic choices on communication to be examined.

Predictions

Most of the research on second-language communication strategies has been conducted with adults. The linguistic classification of the strategies used by these adults across studies has been very consistent. But there is no evidence to indicate whether or not children behave in the same way as adults in situations of communicative difficulty. Hence, evidence supporting the extension of the taxonomic systems to the speech of children would be a contribution to this literature.

The claim throughout this volume is that the communication strategies produced by adult second-language learners are not a uniquely circumscribed phenomenon but are the same set of behaviours employed by children and adults in all communication. It can be expected, therefore, that the communication strategies detected in the speech of these children will be exactly the same as those reported in the literature for adults. This hypothesis is tested by comparing the range and distribution of communication strategies collected in the present corpus to those reported in the literature for adult language learners.

There are, of course, limits in the generalizability of the findings. The hypothesis can claim only that these devices are used by 9-year-old children. The strategies used by younger children would still need to be investigated. Some research with younger children is reported in chapter 5 in terms of their ability to perform in referential communication tasks, and in chapter 6 in terms of their ability to provide formal definitions.

The interpretation of those strategies will be assessed by considering the effect of different strategic choices on listeners' comprehension. The search for factors that predict the choice of a particular strategy and the implications of that strategy on comprehension will be used to assess the validity of the distinctions.

Subjects

The subjects in the study were eighteen girls,[2] of 9 years old, who were attending a French immersion programme (see Genesee, 1983, for a review of immersion programmes). In these programmes, English-speaking children are instructed entirely in French from the age of 5 years. Literacy instruction is also carried out exclusively in French. English is introduced as a subject for approximately 20–30 minutes per day beginning when the child is 7–9 years old, depending on the school. Accordingly, the children participating in the present research had been studying French for five years and had reached an intermediate level of proficiency. At this level they are capable of taking part in most conversations, reading age-appropriate texts, and comprehending French in some media such as film and television, although such comprehension must usually be aided by contextual knowledge of the topic.

Task and Materials

A communication task was created which had a 'game-like' quality. Two large boards (approximately 70 × 50 cm) were covered in black felt and divided into twelve sections each (4 × 3) with bands of white tape. Each section was numbered so that it could be easily referenced. Wooden pedestals with slats were used to hold each board upright.

Two identical sets of diagrams depicting concrete objects were drawn on white cards, 7 × 12 cm. These drawings were outlined in black felt pen and filled in with coloured markers. There were three arrays of diagrams, each array containing 12 objects. Hence, the full set of diagrams was 36 pictures (3 arrays × 12 diagrams), replicated in the second set, yielding 72 cards in all.

Each card had a Velcro tab on the back so that it could be attached to the felt boards.

Each array corresponded to a category of item, and each category was divided into three subsets. The three categories were tools, subdivided into workshop tools, garden tools, and office tools; things to sit on, subdivided into household seats, stationary seats, moving seats; and utensils and appliances, subdivided into small utensils, kitchen appliances, and household appliances. The full set of items is shown in table 4.1. The items were chosen because they were all recognizable to the children although the French labels for these items were not known. Pilot testing was carried out with a separate group of 9-year-olds from immersion programmes to ensure that these criteria were satisfied.

The children were tested in pairs. When they came into the testing room, there was some introductory discussion about communication and its problems. The two girls were randomly designated 'director' and 'matcher', and then the game was introduced. Each child was given one of the felt boards, positioned so that the front was hidden from the other child.

The problem was for the director to describe all the cards in each array so that the matcher could correctly position those cards on her felt board. All pairs of girls completed all three arrays, but the arrays were assigned in different orders. The experimenter selected the first array to be used and gave one set of cards to the director and one set to the matcher. The experimenter shuffled the set given to the director and placed them on her board, one card in each section. The director had to describe her board to the matcher so that she could reproduce the ordering that was on the director's board. This procedure was repeated with each of the three arrays. The session was tape-recorded and later transcribed.

Table 4.1   Target items in communication task

I Tools			
Workshop:	drill	hammer	screwdriver	wrench
Garden:	shovel	rake	garden hose	hoe
Office:	rubber stamp	paper clamp	calculator	letter opener

II Things to Sit On			
Household:	high-chair	rocking-chair	wing chair	folding-chair
Stationary:	playpen	lawn chair	child's car seat	stool
Moving:	wheelchair	stroller	wagon	swing

III Utensils and Appliances			
Small:	beater	potato peeler	spatula	wooden spoon
Kitchen:	kettle	can opener	toaster	waffle iron
Household:	vacuum cleaner	hair dryer	record player	heater

Methodological Limitations

There is always a trade-off in research between control and naturalness (Bialystok and Swain, 1978). Research that is carried out in completely natural settings is difficult to conduct and the results are often problematic to interpret. If a particular phenomenon is the object of study, such as the use of strategies for referential communication, one may have to wait days for any spontaneous emission of relevant data. Further, natural data are the product of a myriad of factors, over most of which the researcher has no control, and many of which the researcher is unaware. Hence, for the investigation of highly specified phenomena, naturalistic study is generally an inefficient procedure.

Controlled laboratory study assures the researcher that the phenomenon under investigation will be addressed and that superfluous variance owing to extraneous contextual factors will be minimized, or at least, capable of being documented and controlled. But such research brings its own set of obstacles. The sacrifice of naturalness and spontaneity limits the interpretation of the results as characterizing real events, in this case, natural communication. Further, any task, no matter how well designed, imposes certain biases on performance. The researcher, then, must make an informed decision about the alternative research designs available and interpret the results cautiously within the limitations of that paradigm. Several constraints in the methodology of this study have clearly shaped some aspects of the results. These features will be pointed out in the discussion as they arise.

Classification of the Utterances

It was claimed in chapter 3 that the variety of taxonomies proposed in the literature differ primarily in terminology and overall categorizing principle rather than in the substance of the specific strategies. If we ignore, then, differences in the structure of the taxonomies by abolishing the various overall categories, then a core group of specific strategies that appear consistently across the taxonomies clearly emerges. These common strategies should be reasonably interchangeable in tests of their reliability and validity. Differences in the definitions and illustrations for these core strategies across the various studies are trivial. Since Tarone's taxonomy best captures this core group of strategies, the analysis presented in this chapter will be based primarily on that system. Other systems will be incorporated where a broader view is needed to describe some of the utterances. Tarone's taxonomy was presented in figure 3.1.

Because of the nature of the communication task used in this study, the first strategy, avoidance – particularly topic avoidance – is essentially excluded. All the children manage to convey all the items. Instances of message abandonment are identified when the child seems to give up part of the way through an utterance.

This exclusion of avoidance is perhaps the most important bias imposed on the data by the research task. The effect of this lacuna on the assessment of the taxonomy, however, is not serious. The evaluation examines the strategies that are present in the taxonomy and in the data for their reliability and validity. Missing data, as in the case of avoidance strategies, do not detract from this assessment of those strategies which *are* represented. The gap does, however, prevent the formation of a final and exhaustive listing of possible strategies.

The fourth (appeal for assistance) and fifth (mime) strategies are rare in this data set, but that absence is consistent with other data reported in the literature (see chapter 3). Again, most of the literature (with some exceptions, such as Haastrup and Phillipson, 1983), describes laboratory tasks that may exclude abundant use of these two strategies. In the present corpus, the attempts that involve interaction between the director and the matcher are considered under the category of appeal for assistance, although strictly speaking this is probably a loose interpretation of the strategy.

List of Utterances

To simplify the classification problem yet allow for a thorough example of the classification process, a sample of 78 utterances was selected from the data set. The entire set consisted of 324 utterances, that is, 9 directors communicating 36 items each. The utterances chosen for detailed analysis were selected because they appeared to be representative of the whole set and because their selection allowed all the taxonomic classes (except avoidance) to be illustrated. The vast majority of the utterances not included were close replications of those used in the analysis, and for the most part were paraphrases. There was great repetitiveness in the style of utterance used and the features selected for description. It seemed that analysing the full set of data with all of the inherent duplication would not be particularly fruitful. Some of the utterances used in the analysis clearly fit into two categories. Information about category duplication is provided in parenthesis after the utterance. The utterances are grouped according to Tarone's classification and are numbered consecutively from 1 to 78.

Data

Avoidance

(a) Topic avoidance

N/A

(b) Message abandonment

1 garden hose: *Le l'eau vient de ça. C'est attaché à ...* [3]
   [The water comes out of it. It is attached to ...]

2 garden hose: *Quelque chose qui est sur le mur et il y a un fausset avec un
   ...*
   [Something that is on the wall and there is a tap with a ...]

3 wooden spoon: *On l'utilise pour prendre ... si on mange.*
   [You use it to make ... if you eat]

4 drill: *C'est électrique et si on veut mettre dans un ... Ca tourne et ça met
   des ...*
   [It's electric and if you want to put into a ... turns and it makes some
   ...]

5 screwdriver: *On utilise pour faire ... Il y a des gris, des rouges. Le rouge
   c'est comme on met tes mains au-dessus. L'autre part ça peut faire tu mettre
   les ...*
   [You use it to make ... there are some grey and some red. The red is
   like you put your hands under it. The other part is so you can make
   the ...]

Paraphrase

(a) Approximation

6 playpen: *On peut mettre un bébé dedans. Il y a comme un trou.*
   [You put a baby in it. It is like a hole.]

7 stool: *Il ressemble comme une lettre 'A'.*
   [It looks like the letter 'A'.]

8 rubber stamp: *Le part brun regarde comme c'est une tête.*
   [The brown part looks like a head.]

9 stool: *C'est quand tu assis sur un petit, c'est comme un table.*
   [It's when you sit on a little one, it's like a table.]

10 swing: *C'est une sorte de, tu peux dire, chaise que quand tu 'move'. Des fois
    c'est sur des arbres.*
    [It's a kind of, you could say, chair for when you move. Sometimes it is
    in the trees.]

11 high-chair: *C'est une sorte de chaise et il y a une plate-forme là sur. Tu mets
    les bébés dedans et ils mangent sur le plate-forme.*
    [It's a kind of chair and there is a platform on it. You put babies in it
    and they eat on the platform.]

12 folding-chair: *C'est une autre sorte de chaise.*
    [It's another kind of chair.]

13   stool: *C'est en forme d'une 'A'.*
[It's in the shape of an 'A'.]

14   wheel-chair: *C'est une sorte de chaise pour les personnes qui ne peuvent pas marcher.*
[It's a kind of chair for people who cannot walk.]

15   playpen: *C'est comme un cage mais tu mets des bébés là-dedans.*
[It's like a cage but you put babies in it.]

16   child's car seat: *C'est une chaise pour bébé que tu mets dans la voiture pour tu sois 'safe', sauf* (cf. 71).
[It's a chair for a baby that you put in a car to keep the baby safe.]

17   garden chair: *C'est une chaise que tu mets dehors, dans le jardin, dans le soleil.*
[It's a chair that you put outside, in the garden, in the sun.]

18   calculator. *C'est une petite machine avec des nombres.*
[It's a little machine with numbers.]

19   playpen: *C'est une sorte de boîte que tu mets, c'est où tu mets les bébés pour jouer.*
[It's a kind of box that you put, it is where you put the babies to play.]

20   stool: *C'est une chaise en bois.*
[It's a wooden chair.]

21   high-chair: *C'est une chaise de bébés quand les bébés mangent.*
[It's a chair for babies when babies eat.]

(b) Word coinage

22   wooden spoon: *C'est une cuiller en bois.*
[It's spoon of wood.]

(c) Circumlocution

23   spatula: *On l'utilise dans la cuisine si on fait des crêpes ou quelque choses et on veut la prender, on l'utilise ça.*
[You use it in the kitchen if you make pancakes or something and you want to pick them up, you use this.]

24   can opener: *Quelque chose que tu utilises dans la cuisine quand tu veux ouvrir des bouteilles.*
[Something you use in the kitchen when you want to open bottles.]

25   spatula: *Quelque chose que tu utilises souvent pour enlever quelque chose.*
[Something that you use often for picking up something.]

26   hair dryer: *Quelque chose que tu utilises quand tes cheveux sont mouillés et que tu veux que ça va sec.*
[Something that you use when your hair is wet and you want to dry it.]

27 vacuum cleaner: *Quelque chose que tu utilises quand tu veux nettoyer les choses.*
[Something you use when you want to clean things.]

28 wheel-chair: *Quelque chose que les personnes handicappés assis dedans.*
[Something that handicapped people sit in.]

29 shovel: *Quelque chose que tu utilises sur la plage.*
[Something you use on the beach.]

30 calculator: *Quelque chose pour faire l'addition, subtraction, multiplication, et division.*
[Something you use to add, subtract, multiply, and divide.]

31 screwdriver: *Quelque chose que tu utilises pour mettre les clous.*
[Something you use to put in nails.]

32 rubber stamp: *Il y a d'encre et tu mets sur les papiers.*
[There is ink and you put it on papers.]

33 rake: *Quelque chose que tu utilises pour ramasser les feuilles.*
[Something you use to gather leaves.]

34 drill: *Quelque chose que tu utilises pour faire des trous.*
[Something you use to make holes.]

35 kettle: *On met si on veut faire du thé ou du café.*
[You take it if you want to make tea or coffee.]

36 high-chair: *On met un bébé dedans quand il mange.*
[You put a baby in it when he eats.]

37 garden chair: *De fois on le met dehors quand le soleil brille, ou sur la plage.*
[Sometimes you put it outside when the sun shines, or on the beach.]

38 wheel-chair: *Il y a des roues noires. On assis de sur si tu ne peux pas marcher.*
[It has black wheels. You sit in it if you cannot walk.]

39 stroller: *On met un bébé dedans. Il y a des roues noires.*
[You put a baby in it. There are black wheels.]

40 swing: *Il y a des fois au parc mais cette fois c'est sur un arbre.*
[They are sometimes in a park, but this time it is in a tree.]

41 calculator: *Il y a des nombres et on peut l'utiliser pour multiplier.*
[There are numbers and you can use it to multiply.]

42 garden hose: *Quand tu as un jardin et tu veux que le jardin a de l'eau.*
[When you have a garden and you want the garden to have water.]

43 paper clamp: *Quand tu as des papiers et tu veux que tu les laisse ensemble.*
[When you have papers and you want them to stay together.]

44 potato peeler: *C'est quand tu as un patate et tu veux enlever la peau.*
[It's when you have a potato and you want to take off the skin.]

45 wheel-chair: *C'est quand quelqu'un ne peut pas marcher et il s'asseoir dans une chaise et ça roule.*
[It's when someone cannot walk and he sits in a chair and it rolls.]

46 playpen: *C'est quand tu mets un bébé dans comme une petite boîte et il joue.*
[It's when you put a baby in like a little box and he plays.]

47 drill: *Quand tu as une piece de bois et tu veux faire un trou dans le bois.*
[When you have a piece of wood and you want to make a hole in the wood.]

48 wrench: *C'est une petite chose en métal. Il y a les deux trous toute en haute et tu l'utilises avec des clous (comme les clous).*
[It's a small metal thing. There are two holes at the top and you use it with nails (like nails).]

49 hammer: *Il y a un grand baton et quelque chose de métal là sur. Et tu frappes des clous.*
[There is a big handle and something metal on it. And you bang nails.]

50 shovel: *On utilise pour enlever quelque chose. Tu souvent utilises dehors ou à la plage. Tu peux faire des trous avec.*
[You use it to lift something. You often use it outside or on the beach. You can make holes with it.]

51 garden hose: *C'est quelque chose que l'eau peut sortir de.*
[It's something that water can come out of.]

52 paper clamp: *C'est pour mettre des papiers ensembles.*
[It's to keep papers together.]

53 wooden spoon: *C'est fait en bois et on l'utilise si on veut faire de gâteau.*
[It's made of wood and you use it if you want to make a cake.]

54 swing: *Tu attaches sur un arbre.*
[You attach it to a tree.]

55 garden chair: *Si on veut aller dehors et s'asseoir dans le soleil.*
[If you want to go outside and sit in the sun.]

56 playpen: *C'est quand un bébé veut jouer.*
[It's when a baby wants to play.]

57 stool: *Tu peux s'asseoir.*
[You can sit on it.]

58 paper clamp: *Quand tu veux garder des papiers ensembles, tu l'utilises.*
[When you want to keep papers together, you use it.]

59 hammer: *Pour les clous.*
[For nails.]

60 folding-chair: *C'est une autre sorte de chaise.*
[It's another kind of chair.]

Conscious Transfer

(a) Literal Translation

61 wagon: *Tu peux mettre des animaux ou des personnes dans et tu le tire.*
[You can put animals or people in it and you pull it.]

62 beater: *C'est pour si on veut 'mixer'.*
[It's for if you want to mix.]

63 record player: *On peut mettre des disques sur.*
[You can put records on it.]

64 record player. *Tu mets un 'record' sur.*
[You put a record on it.]

65 can opener. *C'est quand tu as une petite bouteille et il y a une machine et tu veux ouvrir la.*
[It's when you have a little bottle and there is a machine and you can open it.]

66 wing chair. *Quelque chose que tu peux assis dedans. C'est très douce.*
[Something that you can sit in. It's very soft.]

67 swing: *Quelque chose que tu balance sur.*
[Something that you can swing on.]

68 folding-chair: *Quelque chose que tu assises sur et ça peux aller plat. Tu peux le mettre dans ta main et la porter quelque part.*
[Something that you can sit in and that can go flat. You can put it in your hand and carry it anywhere.]

(b) Language Switch

69 wrench: *Quand tu as quelque chose qui est 'stuck'. Quand on a une bouteille du jus ou quelque chose et puis on veut ouvrir la petite chose qui est sur la bouteille.*
[When you have something that is stuck. When you have a bottle of juice or something and then you want to open the little thing that is on the bottle.]

70 swing: *C'est une sorte de, tu peux dire, chaise que quand tu 'move'. Des fois c'est sur des arbres.*
[It's a kind of, you could say, chair for when you move. Sometimes it is in the trees.]

71   child's car seat: *C'est une chaise pour bébé que tu mets dans la voiture pour tu sois 'safe', sauf.* (cf. 16)
     [It's a chair for a baby that you put in a car to keep you safe.]

72   can opener: *C'est pour les . . . tu ouvres les . . . Il y a une 'magnet'.*
     [It's for the . . . you open the . . . There is a magnet.]

73   record player: *Tu mets un 'record' sur.*
     [You put a record on it.]

74   can opener: *C'est un object que tu . . . tu ouvres des, 'tins', des boîtes en métal.*
     [It's something that you . . . you open the, tins, the metal boxes.]

Appeal for Assistance (Interactive)

75   spatula: Director — *Tu l'utilises pour cuire.*
     [You use it for cooking.]
     Matcher — *Qu'est-ce que tu cuire avec ça?*
     [What do you cook with it?]
     Director — *Tu peux faire les crêpes et souvent des oeufs que sont brouillés.*
     [You can make pancakes and often scrambled eggs.]
     Matcher — *Est-çe que tu les ramasses avec ça?*
     [Do you pick them up with this?]
     Director — *Oui.*
     [Yes.]

76   kettle: Director — *Tu mets de l'eau dedans et puis il y a une corde qui est attachée et tu mets la corde dans le quelque chose.*
     [You put water in it and then there is a cord which is attached and you put the cord in something.]
     Matcher — *Est-ce que tu mets le thé là-dedans?*
     [Do you put tea in it?]
     Director — *Oui, tu fais le thé.*
     [Yes, you make tea.]

77   wagon: Director — *Tu prends des choses et tu mets dedans et tu pas pousses mais l'"opposite".*
     [You take some things and you put them inside and you do not push but the opposite.]
     Matcher — *Qu'est-ce que ça ressemble?*
     [What does it look like?]
     Director — *Il y a quatres roues.*
     [There are four wheels.]
     Matcher — *Quelque fois est-ce que tu mets les bébés pour les pousses?*
     [Sometimes do you put babies in to push them?]
     Director — *Non, tu mets n'importe quoi là-dedans pour le pousser, le mener quelque part.*
     [No, you put anything you like in it to push, to carry anywhere.]

78 hammer: Director − *Quand tu as un clou et tu veux mettre le clou dans le bois.*
[When you have a nail and you want to put the nail in the wood.]
Matcher − *Je ne sais pas qu'est-ce que c'est un clou.*
[I don't know what a nail is.]
Director − *Quand tu veux mettre deux pièces de bois ensemble tu as besoin d'un clou. C'est une petite chose en métal. Quand tu veux mettre ça dans le bois, tu as besoin d'une chose pour mettre dans le bois.*
[When you want to put two pieces of wood together you need a nail. It is a little metal thing. When you want to put it in the wood, you need something to put it in the wood.]

Problems of Classification

The exercise of classifying utterances into the taxonomic categories exposes obstacles which bear on the interpretation of the taxonomies. Some of these obstacles have theoretical implications.

Problem of Level and Embeddedness The first difficulty evident is the problem of finding the correct level of description. Although the taxonomies present the strategic options as unique choices, speakers do not treat them in this way. Rather, each utterance betrays the presence of several strategies. This combination of approaches used by speakers in a single utterance leads to problems of classification.

If the utterances are evaluated globally, especially taking account of the purpose of the task, then all the strategies must be classified as some form of paraphrase, the majority being circumlocution. All the utterances, that is, are attempts to say something in a different way. Similarly, all the utterances are in some way 'definitions', a style or strategy of communication that has its own characteristics. (Definitions will be discussed in chapter 6.) Alternatively, each phrase in the utterance can be evaluated separately. In many cases, the individual phrases that make up a single utterance would be classified as different strategies, that is, strategies other than circumlocution and strategies that are furthermore different from each other. At what level of detail, then, is it appropriate to begin partitioning the utterances into strategic categories?

As strategies of communication, all the protocols serve to describe or explain the pictured object. This, of course, is not surprising, but neither is it very helpful in understanding what linguistic or conceptual resources the learner is recruiting. The condition to describe was imposed by the experimental task, but this mandate is not unusual in communication. Most theoretical and empirical descriptions of communication strategies have addressed those situations in which the problem was to describe some object or event for which the speaker lacks a label. Similarly in natural conversation, the majority of these communication strategies are probably used to convey the meanings of specific items or events. At the broadest level, then, 'circumlocution' becomes almost synonymous with 'communication strategy'. It is the various ways in which those circumlocutions have been achieved that has typically formed the basis of the strategic distinctions.

Following the option of greater precision would result in a proliferation of strategies that may confuse rather than clarify important differences. Thus, an utterance such as 18 would be classified as two strategies: *C'est une petite machine* (approximation) and *avec des nombres* (circumlocution). But the two are obviously related and the listener makes a decision about the intended reference on the basis of all the information. Similarly, utterance 10 contains the following subparts: *C'est une sorte de, tu peux dire, chaise* (approximation); *quand tu 'move'* (language switch); *des fois c'est sur des arbres* (circumlocution).

Choosing the finer level of detail introduces other problems as well. The first is a conceptual one: if the proper level of description is these partial utterances, then the notion of 'communication strategy' is considerably diluted as it refers only to very local linguistic products. The second problem is a pragmatic one: the present data set contains over 800 such partial utterances, and there is no evidence that the exercise of individually classifying each of them will lead to results that are any different from those reported for the whole utterance analysis.[4]

Related to the problem of level is the issue of embeddedness, that is, deciding how to treat the combinations of strategies that invariably occur in each utterance. In an earlier study (Bialystok and Frohlich, 1980), we considered the main strategy choice to be the overall intention of the utterance and other strategies to be embedded in them. Although we analysed main strategies and embedded strategies separately, it was not clear that this approach was a satisfying way of capturing the real objective of the speaker. Because of the conflation of different strategies into a single strategic utterance, the taxonomic structure does not seem to capture the level of the decision regarding choice of strategy that is made by the learners who use these strategies for communication.

Adequacy of the Definitions   The second problem in classifying speech data into taxonomic categories is traced to problems in the explicitness of the definition provided for each strategy. To what extent do the definitions of each different strategy allow for reliable classification of utterances? Taking them separately, each definition can be shown to contain some ambiguity.

1   Message abandonment: although the structure of the task used in this study makes *avoidance* improbable, message abandonment does occur in the corpus. Tarone (1977) defines the strategy in the following way: 'the learner begins to talk about a concept but is unable to continue and begins a new sentence'. Two problems complicate the use of this criterion to assign utterances into this category. The first problem is the decision about whether or not any 'abandonment' has really occurred. In all cases, communication proceeds until the matcher is able, one way or another, to determine the correct card to be placed. In Faerch and Kasper's taxonomy (1983a, b), restructuring their

equivalent strategy, is considered to be a subset of an interlanguage-based achievement strategy, or paraphrase in Tarone's terms. Thus, for Faerch and Kasper, the presence of linguistic false starts and stumbles is not taken as evidence of abandoning the overall effort to achieve. Quite the opposite: in their view the interpretation is that the speaker has not abandoned anything but has started over in order to achieve the goal.

Examples of the difficulty in deciding between these two interpretations exist in the present corpus. In utterance 1, the matcher might well have selected the correct card on the basis of the first part of the description. The incomplete information about what the object attaches to seems irrelevant, yet the initiation of that sentence determines that the utterance is a case of message abandonment. Utterance 51 provides roughly the same information as the first sentence of utterance 1, yet here the matcher was able to correctly infer the reference to *garden hose*. Hence, classification of an utterance depends in part upon the listener's response and in part upon the speaker's willingness or desire to convey more, and sometimes unnecessary, information. This is a point to which Tarone was very sensitive, as she defined communication strategies in terms of active negotiation between two interlocutors on the meaning of some term. This negotiation, however, is not formalized in the definitions of the strategies.

The second problem is the critical feature used to assign the utterance to the category of message abandonment. The primary basis for this assignment is that a sentence is unfinished or replaced by another attempt before its completion. The unfinished sentences that consign an utterance to the category of message abandonment usually fail at the point at which the speaker requires another unknown lexical item. Thus, in utterance 1, the speaker is trying to convey *garden hose*, but discovers she lacks a word in her attempt, probably the word for *tap*, and that gap aborts the current attempt and initiates a new one. In this case, we would not necessarily want to conclude that the speaker has abandoned the original goal. Rather, the speaker has encountered some secondary problem, and the attempt to deal with this new, and possibly unanticipated, difficulty requires some further manipulation of the form of expression. It may require, in short, another strategy.

Communication, then, involves endless cycles of strategies, and isolating unique ones is neither clear nor simple. Had speakers made different syntactic choices, the need for the unknown lexical item may not have arisen. In utterance 69, for example, the director did not know the word for *lid*, but carried on with an explanation, obviating classification as message abandonment. In utterance 59, the director undoubtedly did not know how to say *hit* or *bang*, so avoided the problem syntactically by simply saying what objects hammers were used for. Similarly, the structures used in utterances 42, 43, and 44 all seem to serve the purpose of avoiding the verbs *to water*, *to attach*, and *to peel*, respectively. The intentions in all these cases with respect to conveying the target term seem similar, yet surface structure differences in the realization of those attempts lead to differential classification of these utterances.

2   Paraphrase: Tarone's definition for paraphrase is: 'the rewording of the message in an *alternate acceptable* target language construction, in situations where the *appropriate form or construction* is *not known* or not yet stable [emphasis added].'

Consider first the criterion for 'acceptable'. To what extent does an utterance need to conform to target-language structures for communication to be successful? The corpus of utterances in the present study is outrageously unacceptable by any criteria of French grammar. Yet the speech is undeniably strategic, and communication has irrefutably been successful. At the very least, all the matchers succeeded in placing all the cards.

Second, what constitutes the 'appropriate' target-language form? The implication is that there is a single identifiable way for reference to occur, and departures from this choice are deviant. To some extent this is uncontroversial − if a simple object has a usual name, then the expectation for referential communication is to use that name. But it is presumptuous to suppose that the common name is inevitably the optimal form. Even native speakers can deliberately choose an uncommon reference for the purpose of explicitness (when speaking to someone who is very expert or very inexpert in a domain of knowledge and greater or lesser detail is deemed appropriate), style (as in the difference in poetic and prosodic reference), or effect (to mark a reference by using an unexpected label or description).

Finally, assumptions about what forms are 'known' by the learner, as opposed to what forms can be retrieved under different conditions, are precarious. There are many reasons why a specific word or form is unavailable to a learner at a specific moment, only one of which is the extent to which that form has been learned. The frustration of not being able to recall a common simple word, or worse, the name of someone you should know, is all too familiar.

Classification according to the specific type of paraphrase strategy is even more tenuous. Approximation, the first type, is defined as the use of single 'high-coverage words' which share semantic features with the target item. Two types of utterances in the present corpus have been designated as approximation: those in which the superordinate set is named, as in utterances 10, 11, 12, 19; and those in which a comparison is made to a similar item, as in utterances 7, 8, 9, 13, 15. But although this difference between assigning the target item to a class and comparing it to a known item appears to distinguish two varieties of the strategy, the distinction is perhaps more accidental than real. Compare, for example, utterance 15 and utterance 19, in which the concepts of *cage* and *box* are invoked respectively. Playpens are neither cages nor boxes, although they share some features with each of these. But the use of the term as a superordinate (box) or analogy (cage) depends only upon the speaker's syntactic choice, 'is like a' indicating analogy and 'is a' indicating membership. The very use of 'is like a' introduces a fuzziness, in that the term is clearly not offered as a single-word substitute but as a form of explanation. Tarone's taxonomy does not attribute much significance to this difference, but others do. Paribakht (1982), for example, formalizes the difference between hyponomy and analogy as different strategies. Many circumlocutions in fact begin with some of the same general information typical of approximation to assist the learner in locating the concept in some domain (e.g. utterances 14 and 11). In these cases, though, the use of these single terms does not necessarily constitute a separate strategy.

Word coinage, the third type of paraphrase, is slippery because it depends upon a morphological/syntactic judgement. The prototypical example of this strategy is usually considered to be the creation by Varadi's subject to convey *balloon* by using *airball*. But was that speaker really creating a word? Varadi (1980) reports the example as two words: *air ball*; Tarone (1977) report it as one: *airball*. What if the speaker had said 'ball with air'? Bialystok and Kellerman (1987) argue that a category such as word coinage allocates excessive attention to a trivial feature of surface structure. It would be interesting to determine whether speakers of languages with more productive morphological systems, such as German, are more likely to generate utterances that appear to be words rather than phrases.

The clearest possibility for word coinage in this corpus is utterance 22. Had the speaker chosen a different syntactic structure, for example, *C'est une bois-cuiller*, the example would have been more convincing. Yet, on the available evidence, there is little reason to believe that it is the speaker's intention to actually create a new word to stand for the concept. Rather, the attempt at description leads to an utterance which is potentially a single word. At the same time, the intention of the speaker in utterance 28 may well have been precisely to create a word. It is conceivable that this girl did not know the French adjective for *handicapped* and attempted to create one by producing a modified version of the English term. The same interpretation may apply to the failed attempt in utterance 62 to generate a word for *mix*. Again, some modification was made to an English word, but this time the result was not the correct French term. Similarly, *opposite* in utterance 71 was even adorned with a French article, but the attempt still failed to produce French. These examples are sometimes classified as foreignization in other taxonomies (Bialystok and Frohlich, 1980). The difference between word coinage and foreignizing is whether the manipulation is applied to the morphology or the phonology respectively. Yet in both cases, if the outcome happens to be a correct word, as in utterance 28, then no strategic devices may be attributed to the speaker.

The category of circumlocution, the largest subset of paraphrase becomes, in some sense, a repository for all efforts to describe, illustrate, or explicate a concept. Many systems propose that these attempts be more finely distinguished (e.g. Faerch and Kasper, 1983a). Some document as well the nature of the description, considering its reference to function, physical properties, contextual information (e.g. Bialystok and Frohlich, 1980; Paribakht, 1985). But such differentiation leads to arbitrary boundaries. It is not surprising, for example, that objects such as hair dryer are described by reference to their function (utterance 26), objects such as swing are described by reference to their usual location (utterances 40 and 54), and objects such as calculators are described by reference to some of their physical features (utterance 41). These choices are appropriate to the item being described and reflect conceptual differences among objects more reliably than they do linguistic ones among speakers.

3   Conscious transfer: Conscious transfer[5] is easier to detect in a set of transcripts than are some of the other strategies, but the inferences made from its use is equally uncertain. Consider first literal translation. The definition and examples provided by Tarone are limited, but the meaning has been interpreted for the present purpose to include utterances in which the structure reveals a direct translation from the first language. Most of the examples in the present corpus concern the position of prepositions, for example, utterances 63, 64, and 67. Utterance 65 takes similar liberties with the pronominal. Although the utterances listed under this category are particularly striking in this respect, evidence of this type of language structure can be found throughout the corpus. The grammar of these children is weak, and the errors they make can very often be traced to the underlying English structure. It is doubtful, though, that such structures are motivated by communicative intentions.

Language switch is straightforward to detect. Its status as a communication strategy, however, is another issue. It is important to note that none of the instances of language switch recorded in this study pertains to the label for the target concept. None of the directors, that is, told the matcher that the next item was a hair dryer. Such a tactic was obviously avoided because it would have been a blatant violation of the rules presented to the subjects. One can only assume that in an actual conversation there would be no such reluctance to make the L1 insertion in place of the important target concept rather than in the place of some supplementary material. Extrapolating to natural communication, one may infer that speakers would make judicious use of language switch as a means of indicating the name of the target object or event. Evidence for such speculation would, of course, require a different kind of research design, one based on natural spontaneous conversation and not contrived laboratory communication.

4   Appeal for assistance: the utterances classified as appeal for assistance in the present taxonomy do not typify the category. The usual example is the speaker directly invoking the aid of the interlocutor through such devices as 'How do you say ...?' or querying the accuracy of some utterance. The present examples do, however, illustrate the way in which meanings can be negotiated through two interlocutors. Faerch and Kasper reserve a special taxonomic category for co-operative strategies, a category that may be a more accurate fit to these examples. Much of the research has presupposed that the listener is an infallible source of authority to whom appeals can be successfully made. In conversation, however, it is often the case that the listener is unable to provide the required term even when asked, and a negotiation between the speaker and listener ensues.

The examples listed in utterances 75 to 78 all led to dialogue between the director and the matcher. If one examines the first contribution of the director, however, it is not clear why this is the case. Each of these first attempts by the speaker is comparable to other utterances in the corpus which were successful in leading the matcher to the correct card. There are, in fact, utterances in the corpus that contained less information, or were less well-formed, but still succeeded in terms of the criteria of the task.

Even when no explicit dialogue occurs between the director and the matcher, there is evidence that negotiation is occurring and that communication is proceeding interactively. Utterances such as 12 and 60 indicate an understanding between the two partners about the context of communication by referring to a previous sort of chair and eliminating it from reference. Clark and Wilkes-Gibbs (1986) discuss this issue at length as one of the 'collaborative' aspects of referring.

To summarize, the criteria for assigning an utterance to a specific strategic category are sometimes vague, sometimes arbitrary, and sometimes irrelevant. If concepts such as 'sharing semantic features' or 'single words' are interpreted differently, the same utterance would be assigned to a different category. These vagaries of classification directly challenge the reliability of the taxonomies and limit their potential for forming the basis for explanations of communication strategies.

Syntactic Strategies in the Corpus

The purpose of the study was to investigate strategies used in referential communication, but transcripts of speech can always be examined from a variety of viewpoints. As a brief departure, then, it is interesting to consider the grammatical strategies evident in the speech of these children. The actual communication task depended on conveying information about the target object, and that could be achieved almost in the absence of grammar. But the children had an additional problem: their grammatical knowledge was insufficient to support the basic syntactic structures required by their descriptions. How did they solve the problem of producing language in the absence of the required grammatical forms?

Several strategies for extending their grammatical competence are evident in this corpus (see Littlewood, 1984, for a discussion of grammatical strategies). The first, which has already been discussed as the communication strategy of literal translation, is to take English sentences and simply slot in French words. There are many examples of this technique, such as those listed as utterances 63 to 68.

The second is a means of dealing with the problem of how to conjugate verbs. The strategy here is to avoid the problem by dropping in the whole infinitive, completely unaltered. This strategy is illustrated in utterances 5, 45, 57, and 75. These are not grammar mistakes of the same order as incorrect conjugation, as the children are probably aware that no attempt has been made to get the correct verb.

The third strategy is another means of dealing with verbs, but shows more effort to produce something correct. This is the tendency to overgeneralize a common form on the chance it will be appropriate for some more difficult term. An example of this is the use of *prender* in utterance 23. The verb *prendre* was incorrectly assigned to the more common and more regular first conjugation.

Finally, a noun phrase can be used replace an unknown verb. In this way, the speaker of utterance 26 avoided the problem of how to say *to dry* by describing the processes as 'to go dry'.

It is arguably the case that these strategies and the errors they were expected to avert or repair are irrelevant to communication. At some point, however, it becomes arbitrary to set apart specific linguistic features as the topic of interest without considering in more detail the linguistic, conceptual, and social contexts in which they arise. Accordingly, these syntactic strategies may ultimately prove to be, not only relevant to, but part of the study of communication strategies. For the present, however, no further analysis of these strategies will be pursued.

Evaluation of the Classification

The utterances obtained from this study were analysed to investigate the reliability and validity of a taxonomic description of strategies and the utility of such a taxonomy for explaining learners' communicative behaviour. Reliability is judged by the distribution of strategies in the taxonomy; validity is estimated by the effect of the strategies on listeners' comprehension.

Distribution of the Strategies

Most studies of communication strategies report little analysis of the results. Typically, a taxonomic system is proposed and illustrated by means of utterances obtained in some corpus. Rarely is any quantitative analysis applied to the corpus to address such issues as the relative frequency of specific strategies, the relation of those strategies to selection factors (see chapter 3), or the effect of those strategies on communication. Yet without such analysis of the utterances, it is impossible to make claims about the reliability and validity of the taxonomic descriptions. Without evidence that the taxonomic descriptions are reliable and valid, it is impossible to make claims about the role that these strategies have in determining the communicative behaviour of second-language learners.

The first analysis of the strategies collected in this corpus was to tabulate the frequency with which each of the strategies was used. The protocols were classified according to the basic taxonomy described above by two researchers. The analysis depends upon a reliable classification of the utterances into the categories, but such reliability is elusive. I know of no study that reports actual reliability data for classifying utterances, indicating the degree of concordance between two (or more) researchers scoring the same data. We did not formalize the exercise statistically either, but disputes on classification occurred for at least 50 per cent of the utterances.[6]

Although there is no claim being made here for the reliability of the final distribution, the data none the less provide a pattern that can be further explored. The utterances were mostly some form of paraphrase yet assigned to different categories if evidence of some other strategy were present within the utterance. Hence, a paraphrase containing a language switch, even though the inserted foreign word is not the target item, appears under the heading 'conscious transfer'. Without this expedient, virtually all the utterances would be designated paraphrase and nothing would have been gained by the process. The category of literal translation was not included in the distribution because the distinguishing feature is a formal error in French based on a transfer from English structure. Such utterances were prevalent throughout the sample and had little to do with the children's communicative attempts to convey the target concept. Literal translation seemed to bear more directly on the children's grammatical competence than on their efforts to communicate. The distribution of strategies across the categories used, then, is roughly as shown in table 4.2.

This distribution is compared to the patterns of strategy use found for two groups of subjects in previous research (Bialystok, 1983). In that study, a group of 17-year-old students who were learning French as a second language and a group of adults who were learning French in a civil service training programme participated in a picture reconstruction task. The subject had to describe a complex picture so that a listener could reconstruct it out of the component parts.

The distributions obtained in these different studies are similar. Most categories differ in their use by only a couple of percentage points. The use of

Table 4.2 Distribution of utterances by strategy

Strategy	Distribution in present data (%)	Distribution in Bialystok (1983)	
		Adults (%)	Students (%)
Avoidance (message abandonment)	4	n/a	n/a
Paraphrase			
Approximation	12	15	14
Word coinage	<1	<1	0
Circumlocution	80	62	75
Conscious transfer (language switch)	2	15	2
Appeal for assistance (interactive)	2	n/a	n/a

the strategies by the children in the present study is more similar to the previous distribution obtained for the 17-year-olds than for the adults. The main difference between the present data and the pattern obtained for adults in the previous study is that the adults made greater use of conscious transfer. The decreased use of conscious transfer by the children in this study was compensated for by an increased use of circumlocution, clearly the favourite strategy. But the overall distribution supports the claim that the selection behaviour of the children in this study is comparable to that of adults who have been examined in other research performing different tasks.

The distribution was examined to determine whether any target object or any pair of subjects behaved differently from the overall pattern. These comparisons were carried out by tabulating the number of occurrences of each strategy as a function of, first, each target object, and second, each subject. A set of tables showing the distribution of strategies used separately for each object, and another set of tables showing the distibution of strategies used for each subject were used for the comparisons. No such anomalies were detected.

Effect of the Strategies

What is signified by the use of these different strategies? The classification of strategies is presumably carried out because researchers believe that these strategies are critically different from each other. If such differences related to differences in the speaker's intentions, then the strategies would have validity. Moreover, the list of strategies would constitute an explanation of communicative behaviour in addition to providing a linguistic description.

Since these strategies are used to achieve communicative goals, one difference between the strategies should be their ability to realize those goals. The use of a specific communication strategy, that is, should lead the listener to form a different hypothesis about the intended meaning. Differences in the listener's comprehension as a function of the speaker's use of a given strategy may be in the degree of refinement of the concept − does the strategy indicate the category to which the target item belongs? Are specific features identified? Can the exact item be immediately deduced? Systematic differences of this sort would be evidence of a valid distinction among the strategies.

These issues were addressed in a second phase of the experiment. The subjects were thirty-two students majoring in French who were in their final year of university. The subjects were tested in groups in their French classes. They were shown each of the three display boards with the twelve related cards. The boards were presented one at a time and the cards placed randomly on the board. The subjects were told that they would be listening to descriptions, or partial descriptions, of some of the objects pictured on the display board and were asked to guess which object was being referred to. They were warned that the descriptions would often be inadequate to make a positive identification, but that they were to guess in each case which was the most likely object. To avoid such response strategies as elimination and random guessing, they were also told that some objects would be referred to more than once, and some would never be indicated. Subjects recorded their guesses on a response sheet that had a column of numbers down the left side corresponding to the number of the description being read.

The descriptions for this phase were selected from the 324 utterances collected in the first part of the experiment. Utterances were selected to represent the different strategies as clearly as possible. As pointed out in the description of how the utterances were classified, most of the utterances actually contained several strategies. These were broken down into the sections that could be labelled as unequivocally as possible (see discussion in section entitled 'Problem of Level and Embeddedness'). Accordingly, utterance 10 produced three descriptions: *C'est une sorte de, tu peux dire, chaise* (approximation); *quand tu 'move'* (language switch); *Des fois c'est sur des arbres* (circumlocution).

The nature of this task prevented all the strategy types from being represented. Avoidance, even in the form of message abandonment, would be an unfair test since not enough information would be provided to the subject to make any reasonable guess. The interactive strategies, conversely, would produce the opposite bias, since the dialogue between the director and the matcher inevitably conveyed a great deal of information. Thus there were four strategies tested in this phase: approximation, word coinage, circumlocution, and language switch. The frequency with which each of these strategies was used in phase one was very different, but for phase two an equal number of examples of each strategy type were selected for testing. Differences in the communicative effect of each of the strategies on the listener would then be more compelling since each strategy is given an equivalent opportunity to be understood. A total of forty utterances were presented in this phase, representing ten for each of the four strategies.

The responses were scored to indicate first, whether the subject selected the correct object or not, and second, whether the subject's choice was in the correct subclass of objects when an error was made. If the strategies are communicatively different from each other, then there should be a relation between the use of strategy and the type of hypothesis the listener makes about reference.

The mean percentage of times that the correct object was selected for each of the four strategies tested was as follows:

Approximation	51.05%
Word coinage	96.88%
Circumlocution	56.38%
Language switch	60.38%

The only significant difference was between word coinage and the other three strategies. Further, most of the errors (approximately 90 per cent) for the three nonsignificant strategies indicated an object from the correct subclass of objects (see table 4.1). Again, however, the strategies themselves did not differ from each other in the elicitation of these errors.

The operational definition of validity adopted for this analysis is that strategy distinctions are valid if they correspond to distinctions in interpretations by listeners. Strategies are unique, that is, to the extent that they imply different effects on communication. In this sense, the results of the present analysis are puzzling: three of the strategies seem to have an equivalent function and one appears to be unique. But what conceptualization of strategic distinctions would group the utterances in this way? Whatever valid distinctions exist among these strategies, they are not captured by the division into the four strategies examined in this test. A further discussion of these data will be pursued in chapter 6.

Summary of Empirical Evidence

Several findings have emerged thus far in the examination of the communication strategies of second-language learners. First, a variety of linguistic distinctions have consistently pointed to a number of ways in which speakers solve the problem of not knowing a word. These linguistic devices have been documented and classified in a number of taxonomies of communication strategies. The strategies listed in these taxonomies recur more or less across taxonomies, across subjects, and across tasks. Thus they must be seriously considered for their explanation of the way in which speakers solve communication problems. Empirical verification of the distinctions proposed in the taxonomies, however, has been weak. Attempts to document both the reliability and the validity of the taxonomic classifications have led to disappointing results. It is possible that the taxonomies are based on incorrect assumptions about the communication of second-language learners. This possibility is examined in the next section.

Fallacies of Form and Function

Difficulties with the definitional approaches to communication strategies discussed in chapters 1 and 2 and the taxonomic approaches discussed in chapter 3 and in the present chapter are certainly different in detail. A weakness of the definitional approach was that it encompassed three criteria considered to be unduly restrictive. These criteria were problematicity, consciousness, and intentionality. The primary criticism of the taxonomic approach was that the classifications lacked statistical reliability and validity. Each of these problems, it will be argued, can be traced to an underlying fallacy which has motivated previous research and theorizing on communication strategies. These are the *uniqueness fallacy* and the *modularity fallacy*. Although both fallacies are to some extent evident in both definitional and taxonomic approaches, the definitional approach suffers more from the uniqueness fallacy, and the taxonomic approach from the modularity fallacy. The solution to both these fallacies, it will be argued, is an approach based on the process of using language for communicative purposes.

The Uniqueness Fallacy

The uniqueness fallacy is the view that the communication strategies of second-language speakers are a distinctive second-language phenomenon. Evidence against this view would be provided if another group of language learners, notably children learning their first language, were shown to use the *same* strategies as those attributed to adult second-language learners. This possibility will be explored in chapter 5.

Even if the communication strategies used by second-language learners have counterparts in the language use of other groups, the problem of how to conceptualize these strategies is not solved. A number of researchers, for example, Corder (1978) and Blum-Kulka and Levenston (1983), have previously acknowledged such similarities. Finding a description of language processing that accommodates the similarities between second-language strategies and other communication strategies is, however, another matter.

The processing of a limited linguistic system by adult speakers of a second language for the purpose of communicating is a form of language use that certainly has unique and important aspects. There are undoubtedly characteristics of this process which are not shared by any other language-use experience. Children operating with limited linguistic resources bear the additional burden of cognitive immaturity, and adults struggling for precision or innuendo in their speech in a first language enjoy substantial linguistic advantages compared to children or to adult second-language learners. But the uniqueness fallacy is the outright dismissal of these situations as irrelevant. Rather, these other special forms of communication should be explored for their potential contribution to the explanation of the communication strategies of adult second-language learners. If our goal is an explanation of communication strategies, then it is important to find descriptions that apply to other forms of communication where strategies may also be involved.

Few data have been offered that enable a direct comparison to be made between the way subjects complete a communication task in their first and second languages. Where such data exist, however, they provide important evidence for the non-unique nature of the strategies chosen for communication in a second language. One such study is reported by Kellerman et al. (in press). Dutch speakers completed a communication problem in both Dutch (L1) and English (L2). The task was to describe an abstract shape so that it could be identified from a set by a listener. The strategies selected to solve the problem were essentially the same in the two languages for each subject. This research will be described more fully in chapter 6.

The Modularity Fallacy

The modularity fallacy is the view that linguistically distinct utterances constitute separate strategies. It is based on the assumption that surface structures are reliably related to speakers' processes or intentions.

In the taxonomies, strategies are assigned to classes on the basis of surface structure forms. The resulting categories, however, are considered to lack psychological plausibility when assessed for their reliability and validity. These classifications, it is argued, provide an excessively modular description of communication. Moreover, they provide no means of relating language used in the service of communication strategies to language used in other situations. Thus communication strategies are modular in the sense that they are generated from a processing system which is psychologically distinct from that responsible for other forms of language use by the same speaker, even when speaking in the same language.

An exception to this charge is the work of Faerch and Kasper, who do provide a model which places such strategic language use firmly within the framework of a general view of language processing. (See the discussion of this model in chapter 2.) In spite of some weaknesses in the model, their contribution is important, not only in the solutions they offer, but also in their explicit treatment of this question, which is too often overlooked.

The modularity fallacy leads to descriptions of strategy use which are based on surface structure linguistic features. Such descriptions are independent of descriptions of language use in other situations, such as communication not perceived as problematic, or other uses of language, such as reading, writing, listening. Modular descriptions of this sort will ultimately be limited in their utility. Carroll (1980) also cautions against the viability of basing descriptions of communicative language on surface forms: 'an adequate analysis of reference may not be able to make much progress if it restricts itself only to linguistic *forms* outside of their functional context' (p. 309).

Conceptual Status of Communication Strategies

Two different approaches to identifying and interpreting communication strategies have been considered: the definitional approach and the taxonomic approach. Both of these, however, are deemed to be largely ineffective in providing a comprehensive description of the way in which second-language learners use communication strategies. Although considerable progress has been made through these approaches towards setting out general parameters for communication strategies (through the definitions) and documenting the variety of linguistic devices found in the speech of second-language learners (through the taxonomies), the ultimate goal of integrating those observations into a coherent account of speech production has not been realized. The next three chapters puruse this intent.

Two research directions will be examined for their contribution to this problem. First, chapter 5 will provide an exploration of the strategies in first-language speech to assess the congruence between those strategies and the ones identified in the speech of second-language learners. This review will consider both children and adults speaking their first language. If compelling similarities are detected, then the explanation of second-language communication strategies must ultimately be consistent with communication in a first language as well.

Second, chapter 6 will survey some research investigating children and adults using a second language. The research is based on a processing approach for classifying observed utterances. A processing approach takes as the starting-point general features of language use that override the characteristic differences among situations and among speakers. Utterances are classified according to the processes that were posited to control speech, rather than according to linguistic variation in the utterances themselves. Empirically, evidence of subjects operating in both their first and second languages offers strong support for the resulting descriptions. Finally, chapter 7 offers a possible theoretical model for language processing which integrates the relevant observations reported in the previous chapters.

5 Communicating in a First Language

As struggling adult learners of a second language, we feel frustrated by our limited vocabulary and precarious grammar. Through the use of bizarre speech forms and verbalization of that frustration, there is little doubt that adults are experiencing limitations and groping to overcome them. Indeed, the majority of the studies of communication strategies have been aimed at describing this experience, partly because it is well documented, and partly because it is obvious and detectable. But adult second-language learners are not unique in this regard. It may be instructive, then, to examine how a different group of speakers manages to overcome formal linguistic deficiencies and cope with communicative situations. How do children compensate for gaps in their knowledge of language and function as effective communicators? Adults also encounter problems of communication when speaking in their native language. Do these situations lead to the use of communication strategies? If so, what form do these strategies take and how do they function in communication? The strategies used by speakers attempting to communicate in their first language in a variety of situations is the focus of this chapter.

The chapter will begin by reviewing the problem of how children manage to speak in the early stages of language acquisition when their vocabulary is limited. The communication problem faced by these young speakers is not very different from the affliction experienced by adult second-language learners who lack adequate vocabulary. Children's use of language in specific referential tasks will be described in the next section. These experimental contrivances resemble the tasks used to elicit communication strategies from adult second-language learners. In the third section, the strategies adults use to simplify their speech when speaking to children will be examined. Finally, the way in which adults manipulate their first language for referential communication will be considered.

Children and the Word Shortage

Children communicate primarily in order to refer to things and ideas that are present (Snow and Ferguson, 1977). The main obstacle to their speech, then, is adequate vocabulary. What children really need to know to satisfy their primary communicative goals are names for things. In this way, children's communication is similar to the adult second-language learner encountering a problem of a lexical gap. Although a guiding assumption in this volume is the underlying similarity between adult second-language communication strategies and other linguistic processes, important differences should not be obscured. The claim in this section is that the communication strategies used by children during language acquisition provide a model for the compensatory behaviour shown by adults learning a second language. There are, however, two major differences between adults and children faced with this lexical problem — cognitive conceptual maturity and access to a well-elaborated lexicon in some other language.

Words and Concepts

Adults may use communication strategies for two reasons. They may have an immediate need to solve a communicative problem — something they wish to express requires attention and effort. Alternatively (or possibly additionally since both goals may motivate performance), they may have a long-term desire to expand their vocabulary. Paying attention to words and their uses may serve an ultimate goal of increasing lexical resources.

Children have a more difficult task. Although they may share both purposes of strategy use with adults, the achievement of these two goals is made more difficult by their having a weakly developed conceptual system. Accordingly, children must shape and develop their conceptual knowledge at the same time as they are attempting to increase their vocabulary. Children, that is, are not only trying to learn names for things but also trying to sort out the structure of things to be named. Keil (1986) has pointed out that in the comparison between adults and children learning some specific skill, one must not overlook the profound fact that children are 'universal novices' — they still have everything to learn. He notes: 'An adult who is a novice in one domain has considerable expertise in others and, if any of these are relevant to performance or learning in the novel domain, the adult is likely to exhibit a very different pattern of learning than the young child' (p. 160). This general lack of experience has obvious implications for children's ability to learn a second language.

The difference between the task faced by adults and children is described more formally by Bierwisch (1981). He distinguishes between two kinds of meaning: *semantic*, referring to the referential properties of the language, and *conceptual*, referring to knowledge of the world. Communication strategies for adult second-language learners are attempts to solve problems in semantic meaning; communication strategies for child first-language learners inevitably incorporate attempts to solve problems in conceptual meaning.

How the conceptual problem influences children's communication abilities is a matter of some controversy. Whether children's inaccuracies in labelling and understanding should be traced to errors in the way in which the world is categorized or gaps in the labels available for the world is difficult to determine. Both an undifferentiated conceptual structure and an impoverished vocabulary would lead to the same linguistic result.

Some researchers, for example, Donaldson (1978), have argued that children suffer relatively little deficit in conceptual structure. Similarly, Macnamara (1982) has claimed that language acquisition can only proceed in the way it does and with the ease it does if the child has a well-elaborated, perhaps even adult-like, conceptual network. Without this, he reasons, children could not even perform the simple task of learning names for things. Some lexical terms that children master quite early, such as deictic terms and personal pronouns, are based on a fairly sophisticated notion of perspective. The meaning for such terms as *here, there, you, me*, depend on detailed knowledge of who is speaking and how these terms change meaning to reflect speaker/listener differences. According to Macnamara, the child's knowledge of the world (conceptual structure) and a desire to communicate interact to allow the child to work out how things are named, including the difficult names for deictics and pronouns.

Macnamara's argument extends beyond just names for things and includes also the syntactic forms and expressions that are the basis of our grammar (Macnamara, 1972). Understanding the semantic difference between such apparently similar structures as *in a box, in a minute*, and *in a hurry* can only be achieved with the support of a well-developed conceptual system that is independent of language.

If researchers who advocate an advanced conceptual system for children are correct, then considerably more research is necessary to determine the relation between children's language and conceptual structures. There can be little argument that conceptual differences mark a significant distinction between adults and children. Nor can there be much doubt that at least some of those conceptual differences are linguistically relevant. But there is considerable debate about the nature of the child's cognitive system and the way it determines (or perhaps follows from) the child's mastery of language. Much current research is aimed at demonstrating that the child is more advanced than previous theorists (notably Piaget) had allowed (e.g. Gelman and Baillargeon, 1983). The way in which conceptual and linguistic structures interact to produce the communication strategies children use is an unresolved issue which must be considered when using children's L1 strategies as a model for understanding adult's L2 strategies.

More Language and More Languages

The second difference between adults and children is that adults know more language. Second-language learners have access to some other linguistic system, and this system can be incorporated into a conversation to replace words, phrases, or structures that are not known in the target language. These strategies have been given such labels as 'language switch' and 'foreignization'. Additionally, adults generally have enough language and enough experience to ask for help in appropriate ways, using a strategy some have called 'appeal for assistance'. But strategies based on language transfer from a native language are probably the most obvious way to stretch the limited resources in one language by relying on those of another language. Language transfer is currently an issue of theoretical and practical interest in studies of second-language acquisition and use (Selinker and Gass, 1983; Kellerman and Sharwood Smith, 1986). In addition, adults may simply know more of the target language, allowing them, one could argue, greater flexibility and choice in finding alternatives and explanations. These differences in simply the amount of language an adult knows (even when that amount is the sum of knowledge spread over two or more languages) undoubtedly lead to differences in the style and success with which communication in a weak language can proceed.

It may be that this difference between adults and children in the number and extent of available linguistic systems does not pose a serious deterrent to communication. Although children do not have another language to rely on, they do have other symbol systems and other forms of communication. Strategies using gesture, facial expression, and manipulated versions of known forms may replace those strategies which adults typically base on their knowledge of another language (cf. Bruner, 1974/5). Although adults, too, use a variety of these paralinguistic strategies, their use by children is probably more frequent and less socially marked.

Differences between adult second-language learners and child first-language learners are not always so simple. Children, too, are often in a second-language learning situation. These children contend with an immature conceptual system yet at the same time have the advantage of another language. How these children cope with the word shortage is a unique and interesting problem (see McLaughlin, 1978).

A recent study by Rescorla and Okuda (1987) of a 5-year-old Japanese girl learning English provides a good example of this process of second-language learning by a young child. Consistent with earlier descriptions that assigned a prominent role to prefabricated routines (Hakuta, 1976; Wong Fillmore, 1979), the child in this study made extensive use of patterns, or modules, which served as frames. These frames were manipulated by substituting new lexical items into given slots, creating long sentence units from simple modules. They call this process *modular chunking*.

Such chunking may be an important example of a strategy children use to exploit a limited linguistic system. Are there, then, systematic patterns in children's early speech that may be considered for their strategic role in communication? An examination of early language reveals a number of structures that may well serve such a function.

Strategies Children Use

Clark (1983) argues that children have three options for filling lexical gaps: overextension of known lexical terms, reliance on vague general terms, such as *that*, *thing*, *do*, and creation of new terms to fill specific functions. Other possible strategies are more difficult to detect. Underextension, for example, is not marked in ordinary speech because it does not result in errors. Similarly, mismatch, the choice of another word that happens to be incorrect, is usually considered to be simply an error and not a strategy. It could be argued, then, that underextension and mismatch are not strategic since they do not solve communication problems. None the less, the child may have intended them as strategies but they happened to be a poor choice. In analyses of strategy use, the relation between intention and success is a recurring and vexing problem, yet it is an inevitable consequence of attempting to understand mental processing solely on the basis of speech data.

Overextension   Of the three effective strategies children use, overextension is the best documented. Between the ages of approximately 1 and 2½ years (Clark, 1973), children overextend a major portion of their vocabulary (Rescorla, 1980). The basis for overextension is usually the distinguishing visual properties of objects, and of those, shape is the most usual (Clark, 1973). Although most visual properties are used some of the time (e.g. size, texture, movement), colour is absent from the list. This may be because colour is rarely criterial to object identity but functions only as a characteristic descriptive feature (see Smith et al., 1974, for a discussion of criterial and characteristic features of objects). Moreover, the choice of a particular property forming the basis of the overextension can change across uses. Bowerman (1977) notes that *dog* can be used for *cats* (four-legged) or *slippers* (furry) by the same child faced with different communicative needs. Children's overextension disappears when the child acquires a more appropriate label for the concept previously labelled by the overextended term (Leopold, 1949).

The interpretation of children's overextension is less straightforward than the fact of its existence. As methodologies for studying children's overextension became more sophisticated, moving from the original observational research to experimental manipulation, the full significance of the overextension could be explored more fully. In her early work, Clark (1973) posited that the incorrect use of object labels was direct evidence of incomplete conceptual knowledge for those object concepts. By overextending the term *doggie* to all four-legged animals, she argued, the child indicates that her mental representation of the distinctive conceptual features for dogs is incomplete, including not much more than 'four-legged'. Her evidence for this argument, which she called the 'Semantic Feature Hypothesis', was taken from a variety of lexical domains, including nouns, verbs, and relational terms.

Disconfirming evidence from comprehension studies, however, has challenged the interpretation that inaccuracies in labelling were evidence of inaccuracies in conceptualization. Huttenlocher (1974), for example, showed that children who had called a variety of animals *doggie* in a production task would not accept these same animals as instances of dogs in a comprehension task. It seemed rather that they 'borrowed' the name of a related concept to label one that they could not name. Further, Rescorla (1980, 1981) showed that such overgeneralizations were highly systematic: following an initial period of correct usage, children overextended common object labels to stand as a superordinate term for a set, for example, using *dog* for *animal, ball* for *toy*, and *car* for *vehicle*. If this interpretation is correct, then children's conceptual structures are actually more advanced than we have hitherto suspected, because on most accounts, such hierarchical classification exceeds the operational abilities of young children (Inhelder and Piaget, 1964).

Like Clark, Anglin (1977) also took the overextension data as evidence for children's immature category structure but traced the errors more to a social/communicative experience than to a conceptual one. Assuming that children were limited in the types and numbers of categories they could form, he used naming practices of children and adults as a means of exploring the way in which children divided up the object world. In his research, Anglin studied mother–child dyads to determine the way in which the mothers labelled objects for their children. He found that adults were remarkably consistent in the word they chose to name particular objects, e.g. choosing *dog* rather than *collie*, but *ant* rather than *insect*. In many cases these same adults chose a more specific term (e.g. *collie*) when labelling the same picture for another adult.

His interpretation is that the adult is sensitive to the child's limited taxonomic (conceptual) structure and uses these naming strategies in an effort to be understood. The basis of the child's conceptual structure is functional: the child classifies the world according to the way in which she interacts with objects. Thus, children label the world according to the categories that have significance in their interactions with the world, a concept Brown (1958) originally called 'level of usual utility' and Rosch and her colleagues (Rosch et al., 1976) elaborated and called 'basic level object'. In this view, then, the naming strategy is not only an expedient used by children to identify and label relevant objects, extending those labels where necessary to less familiar or less central exemplars, but also an attempt by adults to present children with a simplified world-view. Objects are given labels at a level that is functionally useful, and these labels enter the child's conceptual structure as typical category members that can signify the entire class. As a communication strategy, it is extremely elegant: it minimizes the degree of cognitive/linguistic effort required by the speaker by reducing the number of objects and labels that need to be organized and named, and it exploits the shared knowledge of the speaker and listener by following the simple rule of functional utility in naming objects.

All-Purpose Terms   It has been said that to know what the child is saying, you must see what the child is doing, a claim known as the method of 'rich interpretation' (e.g. Bloom, 1973). This lack of referential explicitness may be a reflection of the child's second major communication strategy to deal with the word shortage. The child chooses in this case to use general all-purpose terms where specific words are lacking. Children's speech is full of vague terms such as *this, that, do, make,* and the like to signify a wide range of specific concepts. The strategy enables the child to communicate about topics that would be impossible if more precise vocabulary were required, but the restriction is that the effectiveness of this communication is limited to sympathetic interlocutors present with the child. The strategy must also be supported by considerable gesturing, especially pointing. The restriction is not devastating to the success of the strategies because of the context in which children's conversations take place. Conversations with children tend to be highly animated, contextually driven enterprises, and there is little burden on the child to confine meaning to verbal expression.

Word-Creation   Creating new words where no term exists is a third strategy children adopt to fill lexical gaps. Much of this process is based on transferring words already known in one context, creating verbs from nouns (as in, for example, 'He's *keying* the door'), compound nouns from nouns for objects (*plantman* for gardener) and subsets (*house-smoke* for smoke from a chimney versus *car-smoke* for exhaust) (examples from Clark, 1983). To a large extent, however, word creation takes the form of using morphemes overproductively to generate new forms. Indeed, the strategy of word creation by young children has provided a rich source of data in children's language acquisition research from which to investigate the kinds of hypotheses children hold about language at different points in their development. The generality of these hypotheses is evident from studies comparing the word-formation processes of American children learning English and Israeli children learning Hebrew (Clark and Berman, 1987).

Evidence from experimental studies, however, imposes some limits on this word-creation process by young children. Carroll (1981) specifically instructed children to create names for things, where the array of things to be named included symbols, pictures, occupations, and procedures. The names were judged for how good they were, using such criteria as how easy they were to learn and remember, as well as how easy they were to generate. Surprisingly, in the whole data set there were almost no instances of purely coined terms. Most names were compounds and phrases in which common nouns were modified. Naming by assigning a new unique and single label to the concept was extremely rare. Consistent with the other two strategies, this strategy appears to proceed by exploiting what is already known and used and extending it with minimal modification to a new situation. The relative lack of such word creations is also reminiscent of the relative absence of word coinages reported for adult second-language learners.

Status of Children's Strategies

Children, then, solve the problem of a limited vocabulary by relying on a small set of strategies to fill lexical gaps. These strategies are employed by virtually all children, and appear in virtually all communicative situations. There seems to be no systematic way of predicting the particular choice of strategy a child will make; rather, the child's present vocabulary in conjunction with the child's communicative intention will determine the form of utterance that is produced.

Is it appropriate to call these devices strategies? Do they bear any resemblance to the linguistic devices used by adult second-language learners which form a repertoire of communication strategies? Deciding on the status of these linguistic devices in children's speech is important if their use is to serve as a basis for describing strategies used by adults.

Clark (1983) attributes strategic status to them because they are *intentional*. Production, she claims, requires active search and evaluation of available labels. Children's strategies are a reflection of their choice to label an adjacent concept when the correct one is missing. Dockrell and Campbell (1986) cite the *regularities* in children's decisions in these cases as evidence that the behaviour is strategic. They insist that the child need not be aware of these strategies (or databases), and that they may be related to either linguistic or nonlinguistic information. These are, of course, extremely loose criteria, but the consensus is that the function of such linguistic selections by young children is to serve as a strategy for solving a communication problem.

Adult Use of Strategies   More compelling evidence for the importance and generality of these linguistic devices is the observation that the three approaches used by children for solving communication problems are each found to characterize the speech of adults. Although we may not be guilty of blatant and erroneous overextension, we are none the less victim to the same phenomenon of naming based on utility that children demonstrate. We have *fish* or *steak* for dinner, although these two terms indicate different levels of partitioning. More erroneously, perhaps, is the tendency to overextend product names as generic forms, referring to Kleenex and Xerox.

An overreliance on all-purpose terms is also characteristic of some adult speech. The effect of nonspecific adult speech on children's comprehension and cognitive development was documented long ago in a study by Hess and Shipman (1965). Their study was motivated by Bernstein's (1961) theory of restricted and elaborated codes. Hess and Shipman analysed the language used by mothers explaining the solution to a sorting task to their children. Mother–child pairs were left with a set of materials and the mother was asked to explain to the child how the objects could be used to form classifications. Following the session, children were tested for their ability to form the groupings and the tapes of the mother's speech were analysed for their 'semantic richness'. The distinguishing feature of the mothers' speech was the presence or absence of large numbers of inexplicit cover terms. Thus, mothers would give either specific instructions, such as 'The things that are all the same color you put in one section; in the second section you put another group of colors, and in the third section you put the last group of colors', or general ones, such as 'Just put them right here; put the other one right here; all right, put the other one there'. Predictably, a child's ability to solve the problem was directly related to the kind of verbal instruction received, the better performance being found among children who had received the more explicit instructions. Communicative effectiveness varied as a function of the speaker's strategy choice.

Regarding the third strategy, adults, too, routinely create words to solve communication problems. Often the neologism is so successful it goes unnoticed, leaving the listener with the sense that if it is not a word, it ought to be! Moreover, being the power-brokers of society, adults have a considerably better chance than children do to get their new words incorporated into the language. Some current examples come from computer analogies, leaving us with (highly dispensable) words such as *interfacing* and *networking*. Children's creations, on the other hand, are generally consigned to obscurity unless one of their parents is either an important psycholinguist (e.g. Melissa Bowerman's daughter, who claimed to *unlove* her) or a popular scientist (e.g. Carl Sagan's son, who invented the word *googleplex* to signify an extremely high number, the number of zeros for which escapes me).

Cognitive Demands of Strategies Any linguistic behaviour that young children engage in will be constrained by their limits of cognitive sophistication. Thus, even if the strategies found in the speech of young children were transplanted to adult second-language learners, there would undoubtedly be important and obvious differences between them. The cognitive constraints that influence children's use of communication strategies limits the extension of the analysis to adults. It is useful, then, to explore some of the factors that constrain children's strategic use of language.

One limitation is the child's normal cognitive/linguistic development. In a study of concept formation, Tager-Flusberg (1986) showed pictures of objects to children who were normal, autistic, or retarded and asked them to label the objects. The objects were selected because they were expected to pose a labelling problem for children, allowing the researchers to study the naming strategies used by these groups. For normal children, 25 per cent of the objects they could not label were given functional descriptions, producing, for example, *cutter* for *scissors*, and *you row it* for *canoe*.[1] A semantic strategy, which most closely corresponds to Clark's overextension (*duck* for *rooster*), accounted for most of the remaining responses of the normal children. In contrast to this pattern, the two disabled groups used the functional description strategy for only 7 per cent of their unlabelled objects. The retarded children provided a large number of errors that could be traced to interference from previous pictures or irrelevant associations with the target picture. The autistic children most frequently chose not to respond when they lacked the correct label. Thus the usual pattern of strategy use by normal children to label objects is not necessarily characteristic of the communication strategies of retarded or autistic children. It is, however, highly reminiscent of strategies evident in adult speech which were discussed in chapter 3. It may be inferred, then, that these communication strategies require both cognitive competence (cf. retarded children) and motivation to communicate (cf. autistic children).

To summarize, children quickly develop a number of effective means for stretching their limited vocabulary to allow them to communicate. Their conversations in the earliest stages may involve little more than labelling the objects around them, but, as we have been reminded by such researchers as Bloom (1970), Schlesinger (1971) and others, these simple utterances can convey a variety of different meanings. It is through the strategies of over-extending known words to use them as metaphors or analogies for unknown words, through reliance on general nonspecific terms, and through creation of new descriptive labels that children can overcome lexical shortages.

Referential Communication

Dickson (1982), in a review of research on children's referential communication, defines referential communication as 'that type of communication involved in such activities as giving directions on a map, telling someone how to assemble a piece of equipment, or how to select a specific object from a larger set of objects' (p. 1). While the absence of specific lexis is not mentioned as a defining property, these tasks none the less share features with communication that is likely to generate a variety of communication strategies. Words must be selected with care, often in the absence of relevant technical language; concessions must be made to both the background knowledge and linguistic knowledge of the interlocutor; and the use of language is integrated into a problem-solving activity. Hence, research examining children's performance in referential communication situations may prove pertinent to an analysis of the communication strategies of second-language learners.

Whitehurst and Sonnenschein (1985) describe children's development in this domain of communicative language use. Children, they claim, begin by acquiring global communication rules. The rules and procedures they develop become increasingly specific, moving on, for example, to rules for maintaining sensitivity to the listener. Finally children develop rules for attention to specific wording and specific properties of the referential array. The incorporation of more of these rules is evidence for new communication strategies. As these rules are added, the strategies shift from simple naming to more complex identification of relevant properties.

In his review, Dickson (1982) surveyed 101 studies of referential communication that appeared in journals between 1972 and 1981. Several findings were consistently reported across these studies. The variety of results and interpretations documented in these studies converged on three issues in referential communication. The three issues were the factors that relate to success on the types of tasks typically used in these studies, the role of task characteristics on performance, and the possibility of modifying children's performance through training.

Determinants of Successful Performance

The most obvious place to search for a predictor of success on a referential communication task is language proficiency. Indeed, a large number of the studies surveyed by Dickson included various measures of verbal performance. The results from these measures, however, were less obvious.

Verbal ability, usually measured by verbal IQ or vocabulary, was not strongly related to communicative performance. The average correlations were in the range of 0.3 to 0.4, not normally considered to be convincing evidence of a relation. Language proficiency, at least as it is usually measured, did not determine the way in which children solved these communication problems.

A stronger determinant of communicative performance for both children and adults was social class. The communication of lower-class subjects was holistic, requiring higher levels of inference on the part of the listener. The middle-class subjects were more likely to give descriptive and analytic messages. This finding was replicated across a range of studies for all age groups including adults. It is tempting to compare these two styles of referential communication to the two types of linguistic code posited by Bernstein (1961) to signal differences in social class.

Other research has examined different hypotheses for identifying the determiners of successful referential communication. One approach is to consider the communication task in terms of its information-processing demands (Shatz, 1978). The argument is that referential communication is a complex cognitive problem, and success with the task can be predicted by a measure of the information-processing capacity of the child. Another approach is to explore the cognitive style differences among children, assuming that more effective communication strategies are associated with identifiable cognitive styles (Ammon, 1981). Both approaches have had moderate success in accounting for the variance in performance on referential communication tasks.

Nature of the Task

Performance in problems of referential communication varied as a function of task. One of the motivating questions in studying children's referential communication has been to test the claim made by Piaget and Inhelder (1956) that children are unable to take the perspective of another person and are, therefore, egocentric. Dickson's (1982) survey revealed that egocentrism seems to come and go as the experimental task changes. Flavell (1977) also noted the importance of task characteristics in determining performance. Attribution of general cognitive dispositions to children (or adults) on the basis of performance in a single task is notoriously dangerous, and performance in communication problems is no exception.

Kahan and Richards (1986) carried out a study of referential communication with children 5 to 11 years old plus college students. An important manipulation in their study was the use of context. The target items were presented either within a context of similar items or without them. They point out that real communication usually has such a context, making the contextualized condition the more natural. Their interest in the no-context condition was to 'push children's referential communication to their limits' (p. 1133). At all age groups, there were large differences in performance as a function of the type of task, the context condition always being solved better than the no-context condition. Again, as Dickson points out, generalizations from such experimental situations must be extended to real communication with caution.

The study by Kahan and Richards revealed an important interaction between the type of task and performance. The strategies used by the children were classified as being a simple naming strategy, or one providing a type of detail. This distinction refers to the use of either a holistic or an analytic (part) description. The appropriate strategy in the contextualized condition is the analytic one, since the simple name does not adequately distinguish between the objects. If all the objects were dogs, for example, then successful communication required pointing out that the target object was *the black one*. None the less, the youngest children, up to about 7 years of age, usually chose the simple name. Older children (8-year-olds) shifted to select the analytic strategy, but it was not until about 9 years of age that the strategy was used effectively, that is, selecting an important descriptive detail to convey the identity of the object. It is only through a comparison of the strategies used in the two different task conditions that the subtle shift in children's ability to select and then effectively use the most appropriate strategy could be detected.

Training Strategies

Finally, Dickson summarized the success of improving referential communication by training across the studies surveyed. Most of the training studies focused on specific subskills, such as teaching the children to be 'active listeners', using 'comparison skills' to note similarities and differences between items, and to develop plans for eliciting information. The successes were moderate: subskill training had some (limited) effect on those subskills. Dickson points out that referential communication skill is composed of a large number of subskills, and the success of training will be inevitably limited. He concludes that there is no evidence that the skills can be modified in complex communicative tasks.

Some of the studies which have successfully improved referential communication have done so by identifying a specific obstacle that was preventing the child from being more informative when attempting to solve communication problems (Pratt et al., 1984; Sonnenschein and Whitehurst, 1984). In these studies, children were taught to abandon inappropriate naming strategies and to replace them with ones more sensitive to the features of the display.

The most pervasive finding throughout the training literature, however, is the absence of an impressive improvement in children's approaches to communication. There appears to be a normal progression in which children become increasingly sensitive to the relevant properties of the display and increasingly able to communicate those properties to a listener. The general structure of communication seems to change little; it is the child's ability to evaluate the properties that will be informative that undergoes the most important evolution.

Conversations with Children

Children may lack lexicon, but they do not lack conversation. What do children need to know about discourse to participate in conversations? How do children stretch their resources to accomplish this? And how do adults accommodate children's limitations when engaging in these conversations?

An analysis of adults' conversations with children provides an important source of evidence for the nature of adults' strategic competence in a first language. If there are specific strategies that adults employ in conversations with children, then these strategies and the knowledge of procedures for carrying them out are part of the adult's strategic repertoire. This repertoire is presumably available when the adult is learning a second language. There is a direct application, that is, from the strategic competence developed when learning a first language to an aspect of proficiency in a second language.

More important, however, is the possible strategic skill disclosed by children during their early conversations. Young children manage to participate effectively in conversations, even when their formal linguistic knowledge is weak. The purpose of this section is to explore the origins of conversation in children and to examine the continuity in the development of communication from the child's earliest experiences. Such continuity would suggest that the basic strategic principles for communicating are part of what the child learns with (and possibly as antecedent to) her first language. These strategic resources, therefore, are available to adults when speaking in a second language. If this is the case, then adults need learn only the language-specific means for expression that correspond to an established set of communication strategies.

Learning about Communicating

Grice (1957) described communication as the process of speakers and listeners exchanging plans and discovering intentions. Searle (1969) amplified this position by identifying the appropriacy conditions of speech acts that makes such discovery possible. In this view, communication itself is inherently strategic and intensely complex. The ability to participate in conversation, or communicative competence, is similarly complex and depends on a range of other abilities.

Cognitive Basis The ability to carry on a successful conversation requires much more than a long word list. As Shatz (1983) points out, 'communication may be essentially a social affair, but it is fundamentally a cognitive activity as well' (p. 842). Children must learn strategies for turn-taking, for expressing a variety of speech acts, for marking politeness, for anaphoric reference, and the like. These devices are strategic in that they represent choices that the speaker must make in the course of communication.

Bierwisch (1980), commenting on the complexity of communication, maintains that it must be described within a 'complex theory of human social interaction'. For Shatz (1983), true communication occurs when the sender takes the receiver's capacity to understand into account and exploits multiple sources of information (e.g. linguistic, paralinguistic, and nonlinguistic). Communication, further, is intentional, although it does not necessarily follow that communication strategies must also be intentional.

To illustrate the cognitive complexity that underlies communication, Shatz (1983) documents the knowledge sources that are deployed in simple conversation. Grammatical knowledge is obviously necessary, but she claims that the grammatical knowledge, to be usable, must additionally contain: 'the existence of an intentional system, the understanding of discourse relations, the ability to apply relevant background knowledge to communicative situations, and the ability to make social inferences' (p. 852). This, of course, is in addition to any social, cognitive, and general knowledge of the world that is required to support a particular conversation. Clearly, participating in conversation places heavy demands on the extent and type of linguistic knowledge that the learner possesses. Restrictions of vocabulary or other aspects of formal linguistic knowledge can only exacerbate these demands.

Linguistic Basis Among the linguistic concepts children must master in order to enter conversations are ways of interpreting the speech acts of utterances, syntactic devices for producing and interpreting a variety of forms, and sensitivity to social forms marking such notions as politeness. The importance of these formal linguistic devices is their function in discourse. In order to carry out a conversation, that is, the linguistic tools that are specialized for that function must be available.

One interesting approach to the study of children's language acquisition that has gained recognition in the last decade is the functional perspective (see Bates et al., 1982, and Halliday, 1975, for an elaboration of functional models of language acquisition). In such models, linguistic structures are considered for their function in conversation – children learn nouns because they want to name things, they learn adjectives because they want to describe things.

In this tradition of functional analyses of language, important research in syntactic development has been increasingly interpreted in terms of the conversational impact of various linguistic devices. Examples of such research are the studies by Ervin-Tripp and Miller (1977) on questions, Garvey (1977) on contingent queries, and Mitchell-Kernan and Kernan (1977) on directives. These studies illustrate how children's entry into syntactic domains is guided and predicted by the kinds of conversations children have. The assumption underlying these analyses is that children have both the desire to communicate and the knowledge of how to communicate; they need only learn the language to carry it out.

Conventions of Interaction Conversation depends upon a set of procedures or conventions that regulate the interaction. These include principles such as turn-taking, topic nomination and maintenance, interruption, and the like. Some researchers favour a view of language development in which there is direct continuity between early interactions and language development and argue that these conventions are available to the child in the first year. Pointing at an object of interest, for example, can be interpreted as a primitive way of nominating a conversational topic (Bates, 1976).

A variety of empirical evidence has been offered to show that children learn some of these nonlinguistic conventions of conversation very early. Some researchers even claim that these nonverbal conversations are the very source of language learning (e.g. Bruner, 1983). By studying the kinds of verbal and nonverbal routines that accompany the earliest interactions between adults and children, as well as those that mark later activities such as book-reading, Bruner has argued that children begin to learn language by internalizing the symbol system used in the service of social interaction. Thus, the earliest forms of communication, such as adults and infants exchanging glances, focusing visually on a common object or 'topic', or taking turns repeating vocalizations, are the humble origins of verbal conversation. Linguistic reference evolves out of prelinguistic capacities for sharing attention (Bruner 1975, 1977). Simple communicative functions involving mutual attention and naming of present objects, then, are easily accomplished because of their support by the nonlinguistic activities of pointing and looking. Freedle and Lewis (1977) pose a strong hypothesis: 'Linguistic behavior has its origins in a general social communication system to which a formal lexicon and grammar are ultimately added' (p. 158). For them, communication precedes language. They argue that meaning is interpreted and conveyed through a structured series of gesture, eye contact, and touch. Children know how to communicate before they have learned a single word.

Clark and Clark (1977) take a more moderate position and identify the didactic functions of early conversation by attributing more importance to the language. They enumerate three such purposes that set out learning goals for the child: conversation lessons, that is, learning the techniques and conventions of dialogue; mapping lessons, that is, learning how utterances relate to the world and can be decoded with the help of context; and segmentation lessons, that is, learning the units of speech by paying attention to the way in which new words are used in familiar frames. None of these didactic goals is explicit for the adult, but the interactions surrounding the verbal activities with children conveniently lead to these results.

In spite of the likely influence of early social exchanges on the development of verbal conversation, the more complex communicative functions are probably not mastered by children for some time. Some of these may depend little on social interaction and hinge predominantly on linguistic development. Shatz (1983), for example, points out that reference to propositional content of utterances is a late achievement. In the example:

'Please tell me what time I should be home.'
'That depends on whether you want to eat dinner here.'

the proper reference for *that* is difficult even for 5-year-olds (Shatz, 1983, p. 863).

It may be that children's contribution to early 'conversations' is wholly accidental. Contrary to the analysis offered by Bruner and others, Shatz (1983) notes that turn-taking, for example, requires little or no control on the part of the infant. She suggests two alternative explanations for turn-taking. First, it may be that the child finds it impossible to simultaneously attend and behave leading to sequential periods of attending, behaving, attending, and so forth. Second, it may be that it is the adult who takes all the responsibility for seeing that the turns do not overlap. The child passively fills in the gaps where they become available. But on the Vygotskian view espoused by Bruner and others, it really makes little difference whether such *protoconversations* are intentional, or if the component abilities such as turn-taking are innately specified. The important consideration is only that these social experiences provide the foundation for language acquisition. In this sense, communication precedes language.

Simplification of Adult Speech

Children's entry into conversation and communication is greatly facilitated by the fact that adults simplify their speech when speaking to children. The specific forms this simplification take are well documented (Snow and Ferguson, 1977) and include modification of the rate of speech, variation in pitch, changes in the amount of speech, shortening of the mean length of utterance (MLU), decreased use of complex sentences, increased reference to concrete topics and 'here-and-now', and use of repetition. Many of these modifications are similar to the adjustments that adults make when addressing foreigners (Corder, 1977). Are these simplifications indications of a communication strategy?

An interesting study by Newport et al. (1977) examined this question by attempting to determine the purpose for these simplifications. Since all children are exposed to some amount of simplified speech, it is impossible to simply compare children according to whether or not they receive such input and then describe its contexts, effect, implications, and the like.[2] Accordingly, Newport et al. collected speech samples from mother–child interactions and studied the *extent* to which speech was simplified. They divided their children into groups on this basis, creating groups characterized by greater or lesser adjustments to speech. The independent measures indexing the extent and type of speech adjustment included a large range of variables such as those adjustments listed above. The dependent variables were attempts to gauge the extent of language development, and included measures such as MLU as well as the appearance of a number of linguistic features in the child's speech. By using partial correlations to isolate the effects of simplification on these acquisition measures, they found relatively little relation between mothers' simplifications and children's language development. The greatest influence on learning was for a few language-specific features that children managed to pick up a little more quickly if they occurred more frequently in the simplified input. There were advances, for example, in the acquisition of yes–no questions, noun inflections, and the use of verb auxiliaries for children whose input had been more simplified. No differences were found for the development of complex sentences. This, coupled with an analysis of how speech would ideally be manipulated for pedagogical purposes, led Newport et al. to conclude that the primary purpose of simplifying speech addressed to children was not to hasten their acquisition of the language but to ensure their comprehension of the communicative intention.

Corroborating evidence for this interpretation comes from a study by Bakker-Renes and Hoefnagel-Hohle (1974, cited in Snow, 1977). They compared the amount of simplification that occurred in caretaking and play activities. If language instruction were a goal of simplification, then play would be a good time to impose an implicit language curriculum. If communication were the goal and comprehension the major concern, then caretaking would be accompanied by more simplification since comprehension is more imperative. They took speech samples of mothers talking to children during a variety of free play and caretaking situations and analysed the speech for the presence of the usual markers of simplification. The results showed an increase in mothers' simplification of speech during caretaking, and this they interpret as evidence that simplification is a communication strategy employed to facilitate comprehension when communicating with unskilled speakers.

Strategies for Conversation

Conversation and communication are fundamental to language learning. They provide the context within which children learn their first language and are the main forum in which many adults exercise a second language. The principles (strategies) for communicating in these situations are the same. By the age of about 5 or 6 years, children know a great deal about communication, and this remains an important part of their linguistic competence. Adults rely on this same competence when they learn and communicate in a second language. There is no doubt that adults use these strategies more effectively, more efficiently, and more flexibly than children do, but there is no evidence that the strategies themselves are any different. They work just as well for adults. Children do not think about them, but adults can and sometimes do. Whether this reflection provides a critical difference that sets the adult's strategies apart from those of children is an issue to which we shall return. But the very use of these strategies in children's conversations makes children's first-language acquisition a strategic process built from the desire to communicate.

Charades and Other Games

Adults are often in situations in which a word fails to appear or a conversation is momentarily disrupted by some lapse. The most familiar of these occasions is the 'tip-of-the-tongue' phenomenon (Brown and McNeill, 1986). In these situations, a speaker is suddenly incapable of retrieving all or part of some necessary word or concept and conversation is disrupted. The research evidence for a variety of communication lapses of this type has primarily focused on the occasions that signal such gaps, the partial recall that is possible, and the kinds of repairs that are made (Schegloff et al., 1977). The compensatory strategies that speakers might use in these situations (repair notwithstanding) have been less well examined. Yet a rich variety of situations offer the opportunity for studying communication in this form. In addition to natural conversation, these include games in which a word gap is actually created by the rules of a game (for example, charades or password) and experimental situations involving communication. In these cases, it is possible to examine the communication strategies that adult native speakers adopt in their native language to replace a missing word.

Early attempts to study communication in laboratory settings were carried out by Krauss and Weinheimer (1964, 1966, 1967). They developed a task in which (adult) subjects were required to communicate the identity of an abstract figure to another subject. The abstract figure, such as one of those shown in figure 5.1, was presented to one subject who had to describe it to another so that the exact figure could be selected from an array of options. The descriptions used by the speaker during this process provided the data for analysis.

More recent work using this paradigm has been carried out by Clark and Wilkes-Gibbs (1986), whose intention was to interpret adults' references to these abstract figures within a communication model. Their contention was

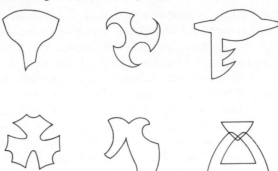

Figure 5.1 Abstract figures for communication task. From R. M. Krauss and S. Weinheimer, Changes in reference phrases as a function of frequency of usage in social interaction. *Psychonomic Science*, 1, 113. Reprinted by permission of Psychonomic Society, Inc.

that communication is a 'collaborative process' in which the speaker and listener negotiate reference. The study involved pairs of subjects in which one of the pair (the director) had to convey a particular ordering for the set of twelve figures to the other subject (the matcher). The utterances used by both partners were analysed extensively to answer a variety of questions about the structure of the communication and the linguistic forms of reference chosen.

Subjects (directors) began the interactions by describing the figures and identifying their critical features for the matchers so that the speaker and listener would have a common perspective within which to refer to each figure. The descriptions could be based on resemblances ('It looks like a . . .'), categorization ('It is a . . .'), attribution ('It has a . . .'), or action ('It is doing . . .'). These descriptions became nominalized so that subsequent reference to that figure named only the feature isolated by the description. This strategy was of course predicated on the assumption that the original description led to successful identification by the listener (matcher).

The descriptions of these figures by the directors were realized through two different perspectives. The first of these is the *analogical* and refers to a description of the figure as a whole. The second is the *literal* and refers to a description comprised of a list of the segments of the figure and their spatial arrangement. Clark and Wilkes-Gibbs argue that these perspectives have different roles in communication and are differentially preferred by speakers. The analogical perspective is easier to interpret and should be preferred wherever it is possible to use it; the literal perspective requires more effort by the speaker and more interpretation and more inference by the listener. Hence, communication is best served by adopting the analogical perspective on description.

The importance of this research is in identifying the forms of reference used by native speakers in ordinary communication. In extensions of this work, Clark and his colleagues have continued to explore this process, examining the strategies used in such related situations as conversations between experts and novices (Isaacs and Clark, 1987). The conception of communication which follows from this research is one in which speakers control reference by taking advantage of a variety of devices which might well be called communication strategies. These strategies can be used not only to enhance the likelihood of being understood, as in the referential task described above, but also to deliberately obscure the intended reference, as in a study by Clark and Schaefer (1987). Both of these are goals of communication, and both are achieved through the selection of forms of expression that serve that end. These choices are communication strategies.

It was argued in the first chapter that communication is a problem that involves mastery of a specialized set of strategies. This chapter has surveyed some of the ways in which these strategies are evident in first-language communication. Speaking effectively in a first language is no less strategic than is the more deliberate experience of attempting to do so in a second language. Moreover, children learn these strategies for communication at the same time as they learn language.

Adults speaking their native language in situations which make the process more deliberate, as in games, or speaking for special purposes where words must be chosen more carefully, or assumptions about the audience's (lack of) shared knowledge cannot be made, have been shown to use the same strategies as children. Moreover, these strategies appear to be similar to those used by adult second-language learners. One means of incorporating these different instantiations of strategic utterances into a single explanation is to begin with the process of language production as opposed to the product or utterances that can be observed. The utterances of children, adult first-language speakers, and adult second-language learners are unquestionably different. An approach that begins with such utterances, then, will necessarily obscure the potential for constructing a similar explanation for their production. The next chapter explores the possibility of using process-oriented approaches to describing the strategic utterances of speakers.

6 Investigations of Second-Language Use

The purpose of this chapter is to explore research addressing issues in the classification of second-language utterances in which the classification is based on distinctions between processes. This research points to alternative ways of distinguishing between strategies and classifying them. Two research projects will be described, each involving different kinds of subjects and different uses of the second language. In both cases, relevant comparisons with the speakers' first language were documented.

The first research project is a study of children's ability to provide formal definitions. The second is a study of adults using communication strategies in both a first and second language. Part of this last section includes a reanalysis of the data reported in the study in chapter 4.

Process Views of Strategies

It was argued in chapter 4 that attempt to identify and classify communication strategies may be undermined by two fallacies: the uniqueness fallacy and the modularity fallacy. The source of both these fallacies is research which begins with observable data and constructs interpretations solely from those observable events. What is necessary, at least as a supplement to such research, is an approach which begins from processing, regardless of the type of language situation, and incorporates the observable product-level phenomena into those descriptions. The uniqueness fallacy is avoided by considering language processing in a broad sense, across different types of speakers and different types of situations. The modularity fallacy is avoided by defining classes of strategies in terms of process differences rather than in terms of product differences.

Definitions of Words

Consider the following utterance: 'Well, it's a sort of horse, a very small horse, which is very lazy, and if not really pulled can just sit there and not do anything.' Although similar in form and content to the sorts of utterances found in lists of communication strategies, the utterance is in fact the response to an elicitation for a definition of 'donkey'. The similarity between this utterance and the observed communication strategies of second-language learners makes definitions an obviously relevant area of study for descriptions of communication strategies. The relevance is particularly compelling when these definitions are being elicited in the child's second language.

Study of Children's Definitions

A large research programme by Snow and her colleagues (Snow et al., 1989, in press) has been investigating children's ability to provide definitions of common nouns in a first and second language. The project is a study of children at the United Nations International School in New York. The students in this school have a range of backgrounds and experiences with English, and some continue to participate in English as a Second Language (ESL) classes. Only 35 per cent of the students have English as a first language, and many children have learned two or three languages before beginning English instruction. For all children not receiving some form of remedial English instruction, French is compulsory. The children studied in this research range from second to fifth grade. Hence, the school provides a rich resource of children with interesting combinations of language abilities, producing a variety of forms of bilingualism, from which to study the development of specific linguistic abilities.

The focus of the research is on children's ability to give definitions of common objects, such as the example of the donkey cited above. Their purpose in studying definitions is that Snow and her colleagues consider the ability to provide formal definitions to be an important 'decontextualized' metalinguistic use of language. Definition is a formal genre that requires selecting critical properties of the concept and manipulating them according to the constraints of the definitional form. In this way, the task is metalinguistic because it demands an explicit and 'intentional' use of words outside of the contexts which endow them with meaning. The meanings in this case must be examined analytically without contextual support. Their claim about providing formal definitions is that: 'while it may reflect no greater knowledge about the word's meaning than using the word correctly in a variety of sentences, or talking about the real-world referent of the word, [it] none the less predicts better to reading skills and to 'literacy' in general' (Snow et al., 1989, p. 5). Thus the general process at issue is learning to use language in specified ways that correspond to the constraints of culture, literacy, and schooling. The use of formal definitions is an example of this type of language use. For these reasons, the researchers predicted that the ability to produce definitions should relate systematically to children's progress with literacy and certain academic achievements.

Children were asked to give definitions for a selection of common nouns.

Those children studying French were asked for these definitions in both English and French, permitting comparison of a specific aspect of language proficiency across two languages. The definitions were scored on a number of criteria, and these scores were related to children's oral language proficiency, reading and literacy skills, and school achievement.

Classification of Definitions

The definitions present coding problems that are reminiscent in some respects of the choices faced by researchers coding communication strategies. The problems of determining the appropriate level of analysis and the difficulties associated with differences in surface structure forms are also evident in the classification of definitions. Variations in surface forms must be ignored or collapsed in order to make classifications according to some relevant feature. The major focus of analysis for the definitions was the type or form of definition that was provided. The primary distinction is between definitions which are *formal* and those which are *informal*. A formal definition is one which contains some equivalence and superordinate: e.g. 'A donkey is an animal'. An informal definition fails to specify such semantic relations.

The coding system developed by these researchers involves quantifying the definitions within each classification (formal and informal), for their quality and communicative adequacy. To this end, an assessment was made of the additional descriptors, including the use of features, examples, and functions. Thus, a good formal definition was 'An animal that most people use to work ... to make them work for them, or to use ride', while a poor formal definition was 'It's a dumb animal'. A similar assessment of the quality and relevance of the information provided in the informal definitions produced a score for quality of definition. A score indicating the use of conversational features, such as pointing, gesturing, appealing for assistance, asking questions, and the like, was computed by counting the frequency of these behaviours with each definition. Finally, a score indicating the communicative adequacy of the definition was assigned on a four-point scale. The most relevant score for the present discussion is the proportion of definitions which are formal definitions and the factors that predict that a definition will be formal.

Development of Definition Ability

Not surprisingly, there was an increase in the use of formal, as opposed to informal, definitions throughout the years examined in this research. At the same time, the quality of the definition and its communicative adequacy improved as well throughout the period examined. Such trends are, of course, to be expected. More important is an analysis of what changes in the definitions over time and what factors might be responsible for those changes.

What, then, is involved in giving a definition, particularly one classified as formal in the system constructed by Snow? Several of the results from Snow's research contribute to this question. First, there was no significant difference in the likelihood of a student providing a formal definition as a function of the language being used. Students, that is, provided formal definitions equally often in English and French. Second, the proportion of definitions which were formal was determined by a number of factors, but not by oral proficiency in English or French. The results showed that 'children from multilingual homes where English was not spoken scored as high as natively monolingual or dominant English speakers on %FD [percentage formal definitions]'. Thus, children who recognized the need for the formal paradigm attempted to adopt that structure, even if their weak linguistic resources made it difficult for them to do so.

Oral proficiency, as determined at least by home exposure to the language (English or French) was inversely related to the use of conversational features. Children with lower proficiency, that is, relied more on the conversational supports such as gesturing and eliciting assistance. Notice, however, that this was unrelated to the choice of the formal paradigm for the definition.

The quality of the definitions, in both English and French, depended on two factors. First, those children who were native (or very competent) speakers of the language scored high marks for quality, for both formal and informal definitions. Second, those children who were not native speakers but were very successful with the subject academically, also scored very high marks for quality. Thus, quality depends on a high level of proficiency in one of the languages, especially as that proficiency reflects academic uses of the language. Snow and her colleagues conclude that: 'greater proficiency predicts higher scores on FDQ [formal definitional quality] and CA [communicative adequacy], and lower scores on CF [conversational features]. It is striking from these findings that non-native speakers can score as high as native speakers on various components of skill in giving definitions' (p. 24).

Implications for Communication Strategies

From grade two, approximately 7 years of age, children knew that there was a specific language style which was appropriate for providing definitions, and their conformity to this style increased significantly across the years studied. The style, which basically follows the form 'NP$_1$ (noun phrase 1) is a NP$_2$', appears in all the taxonomies of communication strategies. The usual classification for it is as a subset of paraphrase; in Tarone's terms, it would be an approximation. Further, the extra information provided in the definitions and assessed for relevance and quality, such as the description provided for donkey after stating that it is a sort of a horse, would be classified as circumlocution. Thus the structures used for providing formal definitions are the same as those used in a majority of communication strategies.

The developmental point which is clearly conveyed by the definition research is that children are proficient with this form. By the fifth grade (about 10 years of age) approximately 75 per cent of all definitions, for children from all language backgrounds and all ability levels, were formal.

One factor in children's mastery of this formal style is experience in school. Watson (1985) has shown how this style of definition develops in children between the ages of 5 and 10 years, roughly the ages examined by Snow. Watson argues that the increasing conformity to the 'NP_1 is NP_2' structure characteristic of formal definitions is not attributable to increases in knowledge, as the youngest children can provide correct answers to direct questions about the superordinate categories of the terms. Snow, too, discounts simple 'knowledge about word meanings' as criterial to predicting formal definitions. Rather, Watson claims that 'the increase in superordinate terms seems due rather to a change in the way that known information is talked about; that is, it appears that implicit knowledge is gradually becoming more explicit and expressible' (p. 191). Adult second-language learners, therefore, could be expected to have mastered this form of speech as a natural aspect of cognitive development. The pedagogical implications of this claim for communication strategies will be discussed in chapter 8.

The identification of factors which influence the choice of formal style by the children tested has bearing on the study of communication strategies. Oral proficiency in the target language was unimportant in determining the type of definition used. The choice for the formal style was made instead on the basis of academic language proficiency. Oral language proficiency was instrumental, however, in predicting how effective the definition would be and the extent to which conversational support features would be relied upon. These findings are consistent with the research on second-language communication strategies in which systematic relations between proficiency and strategy choice have not been found (see chapter 3). Similarly, Bialystok and Frohlich (1980) report a positive relation between proficiency level and the effectiveness of the strategy for communicating.

Process of Defining and Communicating

The formal style valued in the judgements of the research on definitions was considered to be an aspect of the linguistic processes that become possible with advances in literacy and schooling. These decontextualized language uses, moreover, develop directly from the more primitive oral uses of language; they reflect, that is, the same process of development. 'We believe that certain oral language skills are prerequisite to high levels of performance in literate tasks, both in school and out, and that the skills required for reading comprehension and for writing are probably more easily acquired by most children in the oral mode' (Snow et al., 1989, p. 29).

The skills required to construct formal definitions are available to most children, and presumably, to all adults. The selection of this mode is a matter of cognitive, or metacognitive factors, and the effectiveness of it a matter of the speaker's competence with the target language. Communication strategies, by extension, vary in form with the cognitive and metacognitive sophistication of the speaker, and vary in quality with the speaker's oral language proficiency.

The principal implication of the research with children's definitions to adult second-language communication strategies is in the identification of a process of language use that appears to be common to the two activities. Adults already know how to provide definitions, especially using structures that resemble paraphrase strategies. Further, the decision to use such structures is unrelated to the speaker's oral proficiency in the language. Thus, descriptions of what adults are doing to solve communication problems could be profitably built out of a more detailed description of how children learn to define words.

Adult Communication Strategies

Communication strategies of adults can be examined from the same perspective as were the definitions of words produced by children. The important characteristic of that study was to begin by identifying the critical distinctions that represent the choices faced by the subjects. In the case of the definitions, the important distinction was between a formal and informal paradigm. Children's responses were assigned to these categories by virtue of their conformity to one of these styles.

Research on communication strategies is not usually carried out in this way. Two features mark the difference between the definition study and most of the communication strategy research. First, the categories used to classify communication strategies emerge from data and not from concept. They are bottom-up and top-down. In the definition research, the choice of formal and informal approaches as categories for the definitions was rooted in a conception of what these options mean for language processing. The distinctions, that is, are first made conceptually. These conceptual distinctions were then empirically verified by observing different patters of academic achievement that were related to the use of these types of definitions by children with a variety of backgrounds.

Second, communication strategies are usually classified according to linguistic criteria. In the definition study, assigning the data to one of the categories depended only partly on a linguistic analysis of the definition. Different forms of expression, that is, were tolerated within the same classification category. The analysis of definitions which followed from the research had ramifications for a number of issues.

The process-oriented approach used in the definition can be fruitfully applied to the study of communication strategies. Differences that emerge between such a process-oriented approach and the more traditional taxonomic approaches in the types of communication strategies identified, the classification of those strategies, or the relevance of those strategies for communication would constitute important evidence for an analysis and interpretation of the role of strategies in the speech of second-language learners.

Process Analysis of L2 Strategies

A large-scale project studying the communication strategies of Dutch learners of English has been ongoing for several years by a group of researchers in Nijmegen (so will be referred to as the Nijmegen project, see for example, Bongaerts et al., 1987; Kellerman et al., 1987, in press; Poulisse, 1987). Several methodological features distinguish this research from other similar enterprises. First, many of the studies include native-language control data. In some cases the subjects acted as their own control, performing the same task in both languages (Bongaerts and Poulisse, 1989) and in others a carefully matched control group of native speakers completed all the same tasks (Bongaerts et al., 1987).

Second, testing included performance on a number of different tasks. These included describing concrete objects and abstract shapes to a listener, story-retelling, and interview. The converging evidence from such a variety of tasks considerably strengthens their interpretations.

Third, and most important, the classification of utterances was based on a description of the processes underlying their production. These process-oriented categories were arrived at by a theoretical analysis of the literature on communication and language production and by an empirical examination of the utterances observed for learners performing in their various tasks. As a result, the conceptualization clearly evolves throughout the published reports of this project. The principal change that can be traced is a refinement in the categories as they gradually incorporate more observed data and greater theoretical scope. Although other research has been based on one or two of these features, the value of the Nijmegen project is in their simultaneous examination in a protracted and cohesive programme of research.

The focus of their research is limited to referential communication. More specifically, their interest is in the lexical strategies invoked in communication that would be classified as compensatory strategies by Faerch and Kasper (see chapter 2). Accordingly, they are concerned with *referential strategies*, which they define as: 'the process of the selection of the properties of the referent which the speaker then encodes in order to solve his lexical problem and maintain his communicative intent' (Kellerman et al., in press, p. 4).

Classification of Strategies

The taxonomy developed in the Nijmegen project is an attempt to correct at least two weaknesses they have identified in previous taxonomies. They claim that '(a) there has been a tendency to confuse the linguistic realisation of the referential strategy with the strategy itself, and (b) the strategy has been confused with the properties of the referent' (Kellerman et al., in press, p. 5). Both problems have been discussed in chapter 4 so are not elaborated here.

Their solution is a taxonomy that consists of only two strategies, *conceptual* and *linguistic*. These strategies reflect the only two possible processes that can generate a referential strategy: 'Learners can either manipulate the concept so that it becomes expressible through their available linguistic (or mimetic) resources, or they can manipulate the language so as to come as close as possible to expressing their original intention' (Kellerman, in press).

The conceptual strategy includes two approaches which are frequently combined in a single strategic utterance. The first approach they call *holistic*, referring to the use of a single word to substitute for the target. This approach is similar to Tarone's approximation. An example of this approach is the use of *bird* to stand for *robin*, or *chair* to stand for *stool*, in the absence of the more precise term. The second approach they call *analytic*, referring to the longer descriptions generated as attempts to indicate the target word. This corresponds to most of the description and circumlocution strategies discussed in other taxonomies. In this case, the attempt to indicate *robin* would additionally include something like: *It has a red breast*. Such combinations of these approaches are frequent.

The linguistic strategy encompasses the strategies of borrowing (conscious transfer), foreignization, and transliteration that appear in other taxonomies. Some instances of word coinage also belong in this category. The criterion is that the process of communication has been carried out through some use or adjustment of the linguistic label for the target concept. This strategy, too, may be embedded in a conceptual strategy. *Robin* may thus be communicated in the following way: *It has feathers and a red . . . borst* [Dutch for *breast*].

More recently, Kellerman (in press) has reconsidered the scope of the linguistic strategy. First, he notes that native speakers also use the strategy, for example, when particular words are imported from another language for effect. In these cases, describing the strategy in terms of reliance on the L1 is unduly restrictive. Second, some nonverbal means of communication also appear to exemplify this category and at the same time set it apart from the conceptual strategy. Thus, *mime* is an example of the conceptual strategy, while *ostensive definition* is an example of the linguistic. The point is that mime attempts to convey important features and functions while ostensive simply points, much in the way that switching language does. To accommodate these new illustrations, he proposes that the linguistic strategy be relabelled as the *code strategy*. The change is an important one, as the classifications of strategy types are formally removed from dependence on surface linguistic forms. Two different types of nonverbal strategy are classified differently, the critical features being the process of invoking each of them.

In some earlier work on abstract figure description reported by the Nijmegen group, there were three different approaches identified for the conceptual strategy. They were considered in some sense to be separate strategies (Kellerman et al., 1987). The three are called *holistic*, *partitive*, and *linear*. The holistic strategy is to use some means of labelling a whole object. The partitive proceeds by treating the figure as a cluster of components. The linear is an attempt to produce a set of instructions that perhaps could recreate the object, describing, for example, how one would draw it. In the more recent classification system, the holistic corresponds to the holistic approach to the conceptual strategy and the partitive and linear to the analytic approach to the conceptual strategy. Adopting the system used by Clark and his colleagues (Clark and Wilkes-Gibbs, 1986) described in chapter 5, the holistic and partitive strategies correspond to Clark's analogical strategy, and the linear strategy corresponds to Clark's literal strategy. These differences in terminology and classification are probably due to peculiarities of the tasks used in each case.

Several criteria can be applied to the evaluation of taxonomies of communication strategies. Bialystok and Kellerman (1987) propose three conditions that an adequate taxonomy would have to meet. The first is *parsimony*: the smallest number of strategies that account for the data provides the best description. The second is *psychological plausibility*: some description of language processing should be directly linked to divisions among strategies. The third is *generalizability*: the same taxonomy should equally fit data generated through different tasks and using different items and be equally appropriate to different sets of learners irrespective of their first or second languages. The two-strategy taxonomy appears to meet these requirements.

Process and Choice

How do speakers choose a strategy? To what extent is the choice a function of linguistic proficiency? A review of some factors potentially influential in the selection of a specific strategy in chapter 3 failed to indicate a clear role for language proficiency. Not surprisingly, then, an analysis of the Dutch learners solving a communication problem in both Dutch and English showed that in 164 out of 183 pairs of protocols, subjects selected the same strategy in both languages (Kellerman et al., in press). This finding is concordant with the evidence from Snow reported earlier that children selected the same style of definition regardless of the testing language. Also as with the definition data, the quality and effectiveness of the strategy did vary with the proficiency of the speaker. Furthermore, in studies comparing learners of different proficiency levels solving the same tasks, proficiency was virtually never related to the selection of either the conceptual or the code strategy. In one study comprising three tasks, there was a tendency for the more proficient learners to select the conceptual strategy more frequently on one of the tasks, but this difference disappeared for the other two tasks (Poulisse, 1989). Selection of a strategy was in general not made on the basis of speaker proficiency.

What, then, determines how a strategy is chosen and what form it will take? The referent itself is instrumental in this process. The Nijmegen researchers repeatedly point out the problem of 'confound[ing] the compensatory strategy with the properties of the referent' (Kellerman, in press), an error that ascribes each type of description to a different strategy. Thus, description of function (*you use it for cutting*), description of shape (*a blade on a handle*), and word coinage (*a blade-handle*) are assigned to different categories in most taxonomies. In the two-category system, however, these are all examples of the conceptual strategy. The assumption is that there is a natural relation between the object itself and the properties, characteristics, and purposes of the referent chosen by speakers to refer to that referent. Objects with less obvious defining features, such as *hope, love, justice*, could still be expressed through the conceptual strategy, but that strategy would be adapted to convey the relevant information associated with the abstract referent. Strategy choice, that is, is not determined by the properties of the referent, but the specific information incorporated in the strategy is very sensitive to those properties. Kellerman (in press) claims that the form that referential communication will take for a native speaker is 'determined by the speaker's goal and the need to satisfy the usual constraints present in the speech setting'. Language learners, he argues, 'may have to select less favoured options, but this does not in itself imply any qualitative differences in the way the situational constraints are taken into account, nor in the way the available options are selected in so far as they can be realised linguistically'.

A second factor that seems decisive in determining the choice of a strategy is the task being confronted by the speaker. Problems that require describing a single isolated object elicited a relatively low proportion of code strategies; problems involving story-retelling elicited proportionally more code strategies (at the expense of conceptual strategies); interviews produced the highest frequency of code strategies of the three tasks. This ordering was consistent for learners of different proficiency levels. We shall return to a discussion of these results in chapter 7.

Validity of the Two Strategies

Collapsing categories undoubtedly satisfies concerns for parsimony. One can improve little on a system that contains only two distinct categories! But validating those categories is a different issue. The five strategies in Tarone's taxonomy clearly correspond to different behaviours that learners engage in when solving communication problems. The difficulty is in showing that some of them, at least, additionally reflect psychologically different options. Aside from the obvious linguistic (lexical) difference, is there any other essential difference between using strategies such as approximation and circumlocution?

Children's Strategy Data Revisited The study reported in chapter 4 addressed the problem of the validity of the taxonomic distinctions. Operationally, strategies were considered to be distinct if they led the listener to entertain different hypotheses about meaning. Using this criterion, only word coinage distinguished itself from the other strategies.

The data collected in that study can be reclassified according to the two-strategy system used in the Nijmegen project. Listeners' responses in the second part of the task, then, can be reconsidered in terms of the strategy's classification in this dichotomous taxonomy. Do listeners form different hypotheses about meaning when a speaker is using a conceptual strategy or a code strategy? If different strategies consistently lead listeners to different interpretations of meaning, then those strategies are significantly different from each other. Such evidence would support the claim that the strategies are based in different processes of language use.

Reclassifying the data makes explicit the practical relation between the system advocated in the Nijmegen project and the more traditional taxonomies. Most striking is the consistency between these two approaches: to a large extent the two-strategy system of the Nijmegen project can be derived by combining more specific strategies enumerated in the larger taxonomies. The two-strategy system, that is, does not redefine boundaries as much as it does combine subsets into sets. Thus, the Nijmegen taxonomy might be considered as a 'higher-order description' of the same structures traditionally subject to finer discrimination.

The parallel between these classifications provides more converging evidence that the essense of the large taxonomies is correct − the distinctions marked in the taxonomies are the same ones that consistently emerge from analyses of communicative speech. The main point of argument in the present chapter, however, is that these distinctions do not properly describe the process or intentions of speakers who use these strategies. An account of the communicative strategies of second-language learners, it has been repeatedly insisted here, must identify those strategies which signal real change in the way the communication has been approached and account for what cognitive and linguistic constraints characterize each.

Returning then to the reclassification of the strategy data reported in the first section of this chapter, the one strategy from the larger set that is not wholly included in one of the two strategies in the Nijmegen system is word coinage.[1] Some instances of word coinage are semantic in nature, using compounding to convey critical features of the object. These cases, such as *cuiller en bois* are examples of the conceptual strategy. The effort has been placed in explicating and manipulating the concept and its features. Other instances are direct linguistic manipulations, such as *handicappé*. These cases, sometimes called foreignizing are based on a manipulation of the label. Accordingly, the new categories were constructed from the following cases: *conceptual* included approximation, circumlocution, and semantic word coinages; *code* included conscious transfer and linguistic word coinage.

Having classified the data in this way, the percentage of correct guesses made by listeners as a function of the strategy type can be computed. The mean percentage of accurate object selections by strategy is as follows:

Conceptual   53.72%
Code   78.63%

This distribution indicates a real difference in interpretation by the listener as a function of the type of strategy chosen by the speaker.

Differences Between Strategies   What is different about the two strategies is their restrictiveness. As Kellerman (in press) points out, the conceptual strategy invites the listener to infer the intended concept, providing hints about characteristics, category membership, and the like. The code strategy points more directly at the object, restricting information to features of the object's label. To this end, the present data underestimate the difference between these strategies. Because of the nature of the experimental task, the code strategy was rarely applied to the name of the target object. Rather, it was recruited to convey names for things that formed part of the description of the object in the conceptual strategy. Presumably, in real conversation, speakers would be less reluctant to apply the code strategy to the most important part of the message, in this case, the target concept. One could then predict that, all else being equal, given adequate shared linguistic knowledge and the like, such a strategy would increase the accuracy of the listener's hypothesis about meaning.

The two-strategy classification used in the Nijmegen project is an interesting alternative to the traditional taxonomies. The use of only two categories automatically increases the reliability of classification, since there are fewer degrees of freedom for the categorization of each utterance. This statistical advantage does not imply, of course, that these two are the correct description of strategies. But the analysis of listeners' hypotheses suggests that these categories might also be valid. Moreover, the converging evidence from a variety of communicative tasks used by the Nijmegen group provides some evidence to support the claim that these strategies reflect psychologically valid communicative processes. In spite of differences in the communicative situation, that is, speakers' solutions to the problems were consistent, and the consistency reflected their approach to processing the language. A possible explanation for such processes will be explored in the next chapter.

7 Language Acquisition and Language Processing

How do we use language? What is the relation between using a first language and a second language? What is the essential difference between the various uses of language, for example, conversational, literate, metalinguistic? These are some of the questions that contribute to explanations of language processing.

Communication strategies are an undeniable event of language use. Their existence is a reliably documented aspect of communication, and their role in second-language communication seems particularly salient. Accordingly, accounts of their functioning as part of language use must be consistent with the processing accounts proposed in response to any other aspect of language use. Communication strategies, that is, must be placed within the operations of language processing.

An explanation of how the communication strategies are used that is based in a conception of language processing has consequences for theorizing in second-language acquisition. By integrating the account of second-language communication strategies into a processing framework, there are direct consequences for the ways in which we would then view language learning, specialized linguistic uses (such as language for special purposes), and language teaching.

There are at least two ways to approach the problem of explaining communication strategies from a processing perspective. Each of these places second-language communication strategies in a larger context and imports explanatory mechanisms from a smaller problem and modifies the explanation to account for the broadened domain. The first option is to consider communication strategies as part of a general theory of communication. This approach would entail an analysis of the dynamics of communication, perhaps on the basis of discourse analysis of conversations, a pragmatic analysis of language use, and a sociolinguistic analysis of language use in contexts. In this way, communication strategies would be placed in an interactional framework of language use.

The second option is to consider communication strategies as governed by the cognitive mechanisms of language processing. This approach would entail an analysis of the psycholinguistic processes that regulate language acquisition and use. It is this second approach that will be explored here.

This chapter will describe a framework for explaining language processing in a first and second language. The central claim of the framework is that language proficiency is not a unitary cognitive phenomenon but rather emerges from the mastery of two underlying processing components. These components are jointly responsible for linguistic performance. Learners can be shown to master these processing components at different rates and in response to different experiences, including different forms of instruction. Language-use situations can be shown to require different levels of each of these components for effective performance. Thus, the demands imposed upon language learners by various language uses can be described more specifically in terms of the demands placed upon each of these processing components, and the proficiency of learners can be described more specifically by reference to their mastery of each of the components.

The general dynamics of this model are as follows: specific language uses (conversations, tests, reading, studying, etc.) demand specific levels of skill in each of these processing components; different language learners have mastered each of these components to specific levels; learners may therefore perform under conditions in which the processing demands of the task do not exceed the processing demands of their skill development. This is, of course, not strictly true. Learners routinely extend their abilities by using strategies. It is this extension and adaptation of resources to tasks that formally surpass a learner's competence that is in need of explanation in an account of the strategies (communication or otherwise) used by language learners.

The processing components described in this framework are considered to be cognitive processes that act upon mental representations. This is the standard paradigm for information-processing or computational theories of mind (see, for example, Fodor, 1974; Fodor and Pylyshyn, 1988). These models are based on a computer metaphor for cognitive behaviour called Artificial Intelligence (AI). Strong versions of this approach (strong AI) additionally posit that the processes used by computers to solve problems are directly related to the types of processes used by humans. Evidence for models built in this tradition requires implementing actual computer programmes to model the processes that are claimed to be used by humans. But whether or not such working programmes constitute evidence for the processes used by humans is a much-debated issue (Searle, 1980). Weak versions, however (weak AI), claim only that the forms of processing used by computational systems such as computers can provide a model for the ways in which similar problems may be solved by humans. The main challenge to theory building made by the weak approach is that explanations of processing must specify both the nature of the mental representation and the nature of the operations that are applied to those representations. The additional challenge for developmental explanations, including explanations of learning and acquisition, is to specify how the representations and operations change. Following the weak tradition, the framework described here is an attempt to identify two of the component processes that are involved in learning and using language.

A complete account of language proficiency would be obliged to include more than the two processing components described in this framework. No claim is being made, that is, that the description provided here is exhaustive. Notably absent are the 'fast processes' (Jackendoff, 1987) or 'automatic processes' (Schneider and Shiffrin, 1977) that are typically invoked in most accounts of cognitive functioning. These are excluded from the present account because they are relatively inaccessible to investigation and because they are impervious to development. Investigation of these fast processes also contributes to the examination of different sorts of questions from those raised here, questions such as the difference between modular and central processing (e.g. Fodor, 1983). The present account is neutral on such matters.

The first section of the chapter outlines the processing model by describing each of the two components and outlining the ways in which learners develop competence in each of them. The second section of the chapter applies this model to a description of the communication strategies used by second-language learners.

Processing Components in Language Proficiency

The two processing components which are assigned responsibility for language processing are called *analysis of linguistic knowledge* and *control of linguistic processing*. Each is derived from more general constructs in models of cognition and development. Each is independent to the extent that it is specialized for a different aspect of processing, but each is interdependent to the extent that neither alone is sufficient for language processing. Finally, each of the two components is responsive to different kinds of experience for its development. The experiences usually occur in predictable sequences and to predictable degrees for most children, so the two components develop in approximate synchrony. Special experiences, however, can either enhance or inhibit the mastery of one of these essential components of language processing.

Analysis of Linguistic Knowledge

Fundamental to development is change in the way in which we represent knowledge. An explanation of development, or learning, must therefore account for these changes. Analysis of linguistic knowledge is the process of structuring mental representations of language which are organized at the level of meanings (knowledge of the world) into explicit representations of structure organized at the level of symbols (forms). What is in need of explanation, then, is what it means to organize knowledge of language at the level of meanings, what it means to organize knowledge of language at the level of forms, and how the representations evolve from one level to the next.

We begin skill acquisition by accumulating knowledge, knowledge of how to perform the skill, knowledge of how the skill is related to other types of skills, and knowledge of the information necessary to execute the skill. Some accounts of cognition have made a distinction between these types of knowledge, claiming, for example, that knowledge of how to perform the skill is *procedural* while knowledge of the information necessary to the skill, or data base, is *declarative* (e.g. Anderson, 1982). No such distinction is made in this framework: information relevant to performance is not distinguished from the more descriptive information that is incorporated into performance. All this knowledge, it is assumed, is necessary for developing greater proficiency with the skill, and becomes analysed in the manner described by this processing component.

Children, then, learn language by assembling pieces of the system, developing an understanding of the functioning of the system, its role in interpersonal communication, and by improving procedures for using the system, assembling larger stretches of language, and diversifying its range of functions. But the origins of this knowledge of language for children are their experiences in hearing and using language in context. Children understand meanings and can express those meanings; they do not understand the formal structures that convey the meanings.

For several years, possibly as many as six or seven, the knowledge that governs children's linguistic performance, permitting them to speak in well-formed and appropriate sentences, is wholly implicit. Children, that is, do not know about subject − verb − object (SVO) constructions; rather, they know how to say 'Bobby hit the ball'. We would not say, that is, that the 3-year-old child has a theory of grammar. The fact that such young children have grammar at all is inferable only by the behavioural evidence that their speech conforms to the rules and restrictions of such a grammar.

One aspect of the development of language proficiency, then, is making explicit, or analysing, the implicit knowledge that has been governing performance. These structures emerge from the knowledge children already possess about language but have never become detached from the variety of separate meanings with which they are associated. When the forms and structures are represented as independent forms, then the child's representation of language is symbolic. The behavioural outcome of high levels of analysis is the ability to articulate structural principles of organization for the domain. The functional consequence of analysis is that certain uses of language become possible with greater levels of analysis.

Implicit Representations of Knowledge   At the lower levels of analysis, a learner's representations of knowledge are implicit. But how can we attribute knowledge to someone yet deny that they are aware of that knowledge? The claim for implicit knowledge is seemingly paradoxical, yet there is a convergence of evidence from different areas of study to support the assertion that we know more than we can say. Knowledge can be manifested in many ways, and only some of them require explicit representation.

Reber and his associates (Reber, 1976; Reber and Lewis, 1977) have demonstrated empirically that adults form implicit representations of linguistic structure. In their research, adults are presented with letter strings that have been generated from an artificial language. Their results consistently show that subjects can make reliable acceptability judgements of these strings even though they cannot state a single rule of the language, and under some experimental conditions, are not even aware that the strings are governed by a rule system. In most conditions, too, the subjects insist that they are simply guessing, although the accuracy of their performance belies that possibility.

Another source of evidence for implicit representation is in current notions of memory. In a review of the area, Schacter (1987) establishes the presence of a distinct memory system called *implicit memory* by using the criterion of dissociation. Dissociation is demonstrated empirically when two types of tasks, for example, verbally recalling what one has been studying and performing a task which relies on what one has been studying, are statistically independent. The two types of performance, that is, are based on separate forms of mental representation. He reviews evidence from both philosophical analysis and psychological experimentation, including patterns of memory loss in amnesiac patients, and argues for the existence of an autonomous system of implicit representation: 'Subjects demonstrate that they possess a particular kind of knowledge by their performance on a task, yet they are not consciously aware that they possess the knowledge and cannot gain access to it explicitly' (p. 513).

The developmental aspect of this processing component is that representations that are implicit evolve into more explicit representations. Important evidence in support of the construct, then, would be a demonstration that children move from less analysed to more analysed forms of mental representation.

Research on children's conceptual development is one area that illustrates how such implicit representations of knowledge can be used to guide performance in the early stages as well as identifying the limits of this type of performance. Children from about 5 years of age can easily group objects together, apparently honouring such classification structures as superordination (Vygotsky, 1962; Inhelder and Piaget, 1964). Yet, at this point, such hierarchical notions as animal, fruit, and the like, are not represented for the child as explicit concepts. The structures are, rather, implicit in their knowledge of specific objects.

Gelman and Baillargeon (1983) review a large number of studies in which young children were asked to classify objects. Their review establishes that children's successful classifications did not exploit abstract superordinates such as *furniture*, but rather used basic-level categories, such as *chair*. The basic-level category is concrete and observable, and groupings of objects can be made on the basis of physical properties. The abstract hierarchies present no obvious physical basis for sorting. Yet children understand the abstract categories in that they respond appropriately to objects as a function of their superordinate categories. But at the early stages, children's understanding of the formal similarity between say, chairs and tables, is implicit. The explication of that structure does not emerge until the child is about 7 or 8 years old.

Symbolic Representations of Knowledge   It is, of course, incontrovertible that greater proficiency is associated with *more* knowledge. Thus, older children know more than younger children and experts know more than novices. But the claim being advanced here is that the knowledge that older children and experts have about a domain is also represented differently from the way in which younger children and novices have represented the same knowledge. The crucial feature is that at some point in skill development, knowledge becomes symbolic. Symbolic knowledge is independent of meanings and accessible to inspection. For these two reasons, symbolic knowledge can be used for purposes not possible for implicit knowledge.

   The necessity for linguistic knowledge to be represented symbolically can be demonstrated in terms of children learning to read. As claimed above, children can participate in conversations and speak in well-formed utterances on the basis of implicit representations of language. Learning to read, however, requires that some of that knowledge of language has been made explicit and represented as symbolic knowledge. In order to read, children must have several explicit notions of language. One of these is that language is made up of words, and that words are represented graphically by means of sequences of letters. The letters correspond to sounds, and these sounds must have a reality beyond their role in the creation of particular words. The sounds, that is, must be made independent of meanings. Accordingly, children can read only when they have understood the symbolic relation between letters and sounds.

   Some evidence for this progression is available from research in progress in our laboratory. Children between 2 and 5 years of age were screened for their ability to recite the alphabet, identify a series of ten letters, and say what sound each one makes. At the same time, children were excluded from the study if they knew how to read. All the children in the study, then, knew the alphabet but could not read. Our claim is that these children have implicit knowledge of the alphabet – they know it as a procedure that has a beginning, middle, and end – but they lack symbolic knowledge of the letters and how they refer to sounds. Without this symbolic knowledge, children should not be able to decode simple written words or transcribe words into letters. Children were given a variety of tasks involving written letters and what they mean. Passing the tasks required understanding such concepts as: longer words need more letters, words that begin with the same sound begin with the same letter, and a word always says the same thing no matter what kind of picture it happens to accompany. The children in the study found these problems extremely hard and consistently made errors. Our interpretation is that they do not understand that letters stand for specific sounds, that is, that the relation between letters and sounds is symbolic.

The example described above is a rather simple notion of language that becomes symbolic for children sometime between about 4 and 6 years of age. Eventually, a large portion of linguistic knowledge becomes represented in symbolic form as knowledge of structure. Skilled reading depends crucially on sufficiently high levels of analysis of knowledge. In a study examining the cognitive skills that predict reading comprehension for 9- and 10-year-old children, the level of analysis of linguistic knowledge was a significant precondition that was causally linked to reading ability (Bialystok, 1988a). Similarly, solutions to the set of language problems concerned with forms and structures, sometimes called metalinguistic problems, depend on the level of analysis of linguistic knowledge. Examples include judging and correcting sentence grammaticality, producing rhyme, synonymy, or paraphrase, or explaining the rules of the system. Analysis of knowledge is the process of converting the implicit representations into the symbolic representations that are necessary to solve problems of these types.

Consciousness The highest level of analysis of knowledge is associated with what some might call *consciousness*, but consciousness is not criterial to greater levels of analysis. It is difficult to treat consciousness as a determining variable, primarily because the conditions of consciousness seem so elusive. At the point at which we can articulate a principle, it seems clear that we are conscious of it, but it is also possible that it is the articulation that brought the structure into consciousness. In this case, consciousness is not a predictor of the analysis necessary to support articulation, but rather a consequence of it. At the same time, relying on the criterion of consciousness to signal higher levels of analysis would exclude the process of analysis from young children (see chapter 5). Yet young children clearly progress by making explicit their knowledge of language.

Disclaiming that consciousness is criterial to higher levels of analysis is not to deny the experience of consciousness, nor the value of conscious awareness of knowledge as a means of assessing that portion of knowledge which *is* conscious. The point, rather, is that a criterion of consciousness seriously underestimates the level of analysis with which linguistic knowledge is represented. Consciousness is considered here to be an emergent property of higher levels of analysis. An excellent discussion of the limitations of consciousness for defining categories of behaviour is presented by Allport (1988).

Mechanisms for the Process of Analysis Evidence that a process of analysis characterizes children's acquisition of language is based on such indications as spontaneous repairs, errors, and creative use of familiar phrases. Several theoretical descriptions have been offered as an account of these features in children's speech.

One description of children's speech production, based on a process similar to that intended by analysis of knowledge, is offered by Karmiloff-Smith

(1986). She describes the development of a skill as passing through three phases, each characterized by a different type of mental representation. In the first phase, performance is governed by a mental representation called *Implicit*, which is represented in the form of a procedure. A procedure, in this case, is a set of instructions on how to achieve a goal and runs automatically. The procedure is based on knowledge of the system but does not allow access to it. Knowledge, as we generally think of it as explicit information, is actually dispersed over a number of procedures. Thus, linguistic determiners can be correctly supplied with a variety of nouns, but are not organized into a system of determiners; verbs such as *give* and *take* are used correctly without being connected by their reciprocity; and *give* and *put* without reference to their assumptions of animacy. The consequence of knowledge being represented in this form, Karmiloff-Smith argues, is that the performer cannot take out a piece of knowledge upon which the procedure is based and consider it as independent information. There is no concept of *determiners* and no category formed by them. The information necessary to the performance, such as correct use of determiners, is implicit in the procedure, and has no separate existence beyond this function.

Once these procedures and their corresponding implicit representations become perfected, learners attempt to 'go beyond success' by examining, analysing, and organizing their knowledge of that performance. The mental representation then becomes *redescribed* at a higher level — specific features of the representation become more explicit and are assigned an independent representation. These representations Karmiloff-Smith calls *Explicit 1*, and they permit the learner to manipulate parts of the procedure without relying on the whole. Using again the example of the determiner system, she points out that at this second level different functions for the determiner system are available: 'The rewriting into Explicit 1 form makes it possible for analogies of phonological form and differences of function across the multiply-stored indefinite articles to be explicitly defined. Then, the plethora of isolated form/function pairs can be linked, after which one form — the indefinite article — has plurifunctional status' (p. 113).

The final phase, which she calls *Explicit 2*, is a further redescription of the representation of Explicit 1, making the structure itself now accessible. The distinguishing feature of knowledge represented in this way is that it is amenable to conscious consideration.

Other theories of language acquisition also base an important part of development on a concept analogous to analysis of knowledge. Bowerman (1982), for example, attributes a significant portion of children's language acquisition to their progressive *restructuring* of the system as they continually analyse chunks and patterns of language. Concepts such as *plurality* emerge from the analysis of the system. Moreover, this analysis proceeds quite spontaneously. Children's late errors 'point to the importance of children's disposition to discover structure and regularity in their environment independently of any obvious or immediate instrumental gain' (p. 141).

Finally, Berman (1987) makes a similar point and substantiates it with evidence of children's compounding in Hebrew. Because of different methods of pluralizing for single and compound nouns, she demonstrates how young children consider such compounds as *house shoes* (slippers) to be single words. Mastery of the system of compounding and the productive use of the system is not established for several years.

In her description of language acquisition, Berman (1986) identifies five steps to language acquisition, each based on reorganization and reanalysis of the mental representations characterizing the previous stage. The first step is rote knowledge, in which individual items are acquired as 'unanalysed amalgams'. Second is early modification, in which some familiar items are used contrastively. Such contrastive usage implies somewhat more analysis of features than is present in the first stage. Third is interim schemata. The characteristic feature of schemata is that they are organized structures, based on principles of explicit similarity, such as those that become evident in Karmiloff-Smith's phase 2. The fourth step is rule knowledge, evidenced by 'strict adherence to rules but with some lacunae and insufficient constraints'. Finally is end-state usage, in which adult norms and conventions, including the variations of register and style, are consolidated. These five steps she condenses into three phases: pregrammatical (steps 1−2), grammar acquisition (steps 3−4), and appropriate usage. Again, movement from initial to proficient use of the linguistic system is causally attributed to the analysis and organization of the existing knowledge of the system.

Development of Analysis   The responsibility for promoting levels of analysis is attributed to three factors. The first is self-reflection on knowledge. Introspective consideration of a domain of knowledge can sometimes lead to organization of that knowledge through the discovery of structuring principles. Thus we can come to understand the structure of what we already know. Piaget (1971) identified 'reflective abstraction' as one of the two mechanisms of development through the stages (the second being equilibration). Reflective abstraction referred to the child's examination of the logical schemata or structures that were constructed for solving problems. This self-reflection, under some conditions, could promote a reorganization of that structure.

The second factor is the role that literacy instruction plays in explicating children's understanding of language. Considerable evidence links the emergence of children's metalinguistic insights with learning to read, although causal connections between these two have not been clearly established (for different views see, for example, Ehri, 1979, and Bryant and Goswami, 1987). The most plausible explanation is an interactive one, in which a metalinguistic foundation is a precondition to reading, but in which metalinguistic notions proliferate as a consequence of learning to read.

Finally, instruction can serve the analysis of linguistic knowledge. Learners who are in the process of explicating and organizing linguistic knowledge may benefit from forms of instruction which present rules and structures as organizing principles. The limitations of such instruction would be determined by the learner's spontaneous level of analysis, the applicability of the rule to a current problem in the learner's mental repertoire, and the comprehensibility of the rule as an organizing principle for linguistic knowledge.

Control of Linguistic Processing

The second processing component is the ability to control attention to relevant and appropriate information and to integrate those forms in real time. The key component is selective attention; the primary situation in which this skill component is most challenged is when there is competing information and performance requires attention to only some aspects of the information. Language presents multiple sources of information, both linguistic and nonlinguistic, and part of effective language processing is being able to attend to the required information without being distracted by irrelevant or misleading cues.

Since control of processing is constrained by real time, effective control processes confer the impression of fluency or automaticity upon performance. But again, no distinction is being made between automatic and controlled processes (Schneider and Shiffrin, 1977). Rather, fluency is considered to be an emergent property of high levels of control. Skilled selective attention, that is, creates a performance that appears automatic and effortless. The real consequence of high levels of control is intentional processing. When attention can be deliberately directed towards relevant information in the service of solving a problem, then performance is intentional.

Language used for different purposes requires attention to different forms of information, and this attention becomes difficult when there is competing information that must be ignored or suppressed. In conversation, the appropriate focus of attention is on meanings, making sense of the conversation, and monitoring the discourse. Reading makes more stringent demands on attention, as graphemes and meanings compete for importance to fluent reading. Language tests, either for experimental purposes, as in various metalinguistic tasks, or evaluation purposes, as in classroom examinations, routinely demand attention to specific aspects of the language, often requiring unusual attentional strategies. These three language uses, conversation, reading, and testing, impose successively higher demands on the learner's level of control of processing.

The time restrictions that constrain control of processing vary for each type of language use. Conversation imposes a natural constraint; interruptions in the dynamics of interaction disrupt the exchange. Reading imposes a cognitive constraint; hesitation in the integration of information interferes with the construction of meaning. Tests and metalinguistic tasks impose an artificial constraint; time restrictions and response measures demand processing to be completed within exact time limits. Despite variations among the control responsibilities in each of these different uses of language, the common theme is that the learner must direct attention to a specified portion of the available possibilities.

Control over Language and Cognitive Problems The most dramatic demonstrations of the need for control in language processing tend to come from contrived laboratory tasks. The argument is, of course, that processes uncovered under specialized laboratory conditions are precisely the same processes that are used in more 'normal' types of processing, but they are just less observable.

An interesting problem that has engaged psychologists for decades is the Stroop Task (Stroop, 1935). A list of colour words is presented, each one written in a different coloured ink. Subjects are required to say only what colour the ink is, irrespective of what the word says. The finding is always the same: when the colour of the ink conflicts with the word written in the ink, the task becomes difficult and the response times to name the colour increase dramatically. The reason is that it seems to be impossible to *not* pay attention to the meanings. Our usual procedure for extracting information from text, that is, is to pay attention to meanings. The Stroop Task asks subjects to pay attention to colours and to ignore meanings. High levels of control are needed to do this task, and the extra control effort slows down performance.

Some metalinguistic problems used in various kinds of research in both cognitive and linguistic functioning are specialized for their demands on control. The sun/moon problem created by Piaget (1929) is an example of this type. The problem is as follows. Suppose everyone got together and decided to call the sun *the moon* and the moon *the sun*. What would be in the sky when we go to bed at night? (Answer: *the sun*.) What would the sky look like? (Answer: *dark*.) Similarly, the symbol substitution task, created by Ben Zeev (1977) imposes high demands on control of attention. Her problem is as follows. In this game, every time the researcher says the word *they*, the children must say the word *spaghetti*. The first sentence is *They are good children*. The child must respond, *Spaghetti are good children*, and this is very difficult to do. In both these problems, the solution depends on being able to focus attention only on the forms without being distracted by meanings that are either misleading or irrelevant.

Just as low levels of analysis in the form of implicit representations of knowledge characterize children's early problem-solving, so low levels of control describe the approaches to cognitive problems by young children. Keeping with the problem of classification of objects described for children's development of analysis of knowledge, children's performance on these problems is also limited by their lack of control of processing.

The most famous demonstration of the precarious status of children's classification abilities is the class-inclusion task created by Inhelder and Piaget (1964). The child is shown an array of, say, twelve roses and six tulips, and is asked: 'Are there more flowers or more roses?' Until about 7 years of age, the child will answer that there are more roses. The child is unable to consider the relation between the roses and the flowers, because the solution demands dividing attention between two competing (and not obviously compatible) groups. Gelman and Baillargeon (1983) describe the child's limitations as follows: 'the child must be able to attend at once to the part and to the whole, and that is precisely what the preoperational child cannot do. As soon as the subclasses are isolated, the child loses sight of the whole. As a result, he compares the two subclasses rather than the class and the larger subclass' (p. 194).

Another illustration of the young child's lack of control also comes from a task devised by Piaget (1965). In this problem, called conservation of liquid, the child is shown two identical beakers filled with equal amounts of liquid. The child watches as the liquid from one beaker is poured into a third beaker that is taller and thinner than the original two. The child is then asked to decide if the two new beakers (the one original and the new one) contain the same amount of liquid. Until about 7 years of age, children typically insist that there is more water in the new beaker because it is higher. The solution requires control of attention − the salience of the vertical height must be ignored in order to pay attention to the width of the new beaker.

Finally, research in cognitive style has identified a dimension called field dependence/field independence (Kogan, 1983). One measure of the construct is the Group Embedded Figures Test (Oltman et al., 1971). Subjects are presented with a complex figure, such as that shown in Figure 7.1a. The task is to find a simple figure that is embedded in it, such as the one in Figure 7.1b. The ability to solve problems of this type is a measure of the subject's field independence. The problem, in the present terms, requires control. Attention must be directed to the simple figure without being distracted by extraneous information in the larger display.

Recent empirical findings from our laboratory have demonstrated the relation

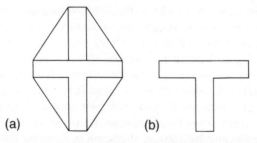

(a)   (b)

Figure 7.1   Example from Group Embedded Figures Test: (a) complex figure; (b) simple figure. Adapted and reproduced by special permission of the Publisher, Consulting Psychologists Press, Inc., Palo Alto CA 94306, from *The Group Embedded Figures Test* by P. K. Oltman, E. Raskin, and H. A. Witkin. Copyright 1971. Further reproduction is prohibited without the Publisher's consent.

between field independence and control of processing. Children were tested with the Children's Embedded Figures Test, a modified version of the Group Embedded Figures Test that is administered to children individually (Witkin et al., 1971), and a variety of tasks assessing levels of analysis of linguistic knowledge and control of linguistic processing. There were strong and reliable relations between children's ability to solve the embedded figures problem and their level of control of processing. No relations were obtained between performance on the Embedded Figures Test and measures of analysis. These findings confirm the claim that a process of selective attention is common to both language and cognitive problems, and is distinct from the process of analysing knowledge into symbolic representations.

Control, then, is the component of processing specialized for governing the attentional procedures necessary to performance. Donaldson (1978) contends that children need to develop control over attentional procedures before much progress can be made in many of the tasks usually associated with Piagetian operational thought. These are the tasks such as classification and conservation discussed above, and children generally master them at about 7 years of age. Control of attention develops over a range of domains, and must also be refined for processing language.

Development of Control   Two experiences seem relevant to the advancement of control of processing over linguistic knowledge. The first is schooling. The logical abilities that underlie success in school performance demand objective examination of problems and selective attention to relevant information, irrespective of ordinary or common-sense meanings. In a study of schooled/literate, unschooled/literate, and unschooled/illiterate adults in Liberia, Scribner and Cole (1981) were able to identify the unique contribution for each of schooling and literacy. They asked subjects to solve a wide variety of problems, dealing with linguistic, metalinguistic, and cognitive skills. Their results were extremely complex, but they were able to sort out important patterns in the findings by means of a series of regression analyses. In this way, a set was identified of problems that were solved better by schooled subjects than unschooled ones, irrespective of literacy. These problems were ones which would be classified in the present framework as involving high levels of control. In addition to the sun/moon problem, schooled subjects were beter at solving logical syllogisms of the following type: All the women in Monrovia are married. Jenna lives in Monrovia. Is she married? Unschooled subjects, even those who were literate, generally answered by claiming that since they did not know Jenna they could not say if she were married or not. Problems such as this involve control – one must focus on the form of the argument and pay no attention to the common-sense meanings that would usually provide an answer to such questions.

A second factor that promotes the development of control of processing, at least for children, is bilingualism (Bialystok, 1988b). Vihman and McLaughlin (1982), for example, report a case study of a 2-year-old bilingual child who could comment on what language was being used, what things would be called, and who could be expected to understand. These are very difficult control problems for most children as they require the child to focus on the language in which things are expressed rather than the meanings. Bilingual children seem to be better at these problems than monolingual children. Because bilingual children have the experience of hearing multiple references to the same concepts, they are quicker than monolingual children to recognize that the form—meaning relation that is the basis of symbolic reference, is arbitrary. Bilingual children have experience in looking only at forms of expressions, as in deciding which language to use to address specific individuals, and in interpreting utterances irrespective of the form of expression, that is, the language, in which they are conveyed.

Summary of Framework   In the processing framework described in this section language proficiency was traced to the development of two components of language processing. Such componential conceptualizations of language proficiency are not new. Bereiter and Scardamalia (1982), for example, have offered a similar analysis for the development of writing skills. They propose that the two prerequisites for skilled writing are 'having knowledge coded in ways that make it accessible, which would mean having it coded in some hierarchical way' and 'having an executive procedure for bringing this knowledge into use at the right times and in the proper relation to other resource demands of the task' (p. 43). In terms of the present framework, the first condition is consistent with analysis of knowledge, and the second with control of processing.

Separation of the two components permits a more detailed description of both the construct of language proficiency and its development. Each of the processing components has its own role in language processing and its own course of development. To what extent, however, does this notion of processing accommodate the communication strategies used by second-language learners?

Processing Communication Strategies

Some of the attempts to grapple with the conceptualization of communication strategies have emerged as more promising than others in their ability to circumscribe and explain the phenomenon. These attempts converge on a binary process model.

Binary Descriptions of Communication

Corder (1983) claims that communication involves means—ends relations: linguistic means are balanced against communicative intentions. When these do not correspond, Corder notes, the learner has only two options:

He can either tailor his message to the resources he has available, that is, adjust his ends to his means. These procedures we can call *message adjustment strategies*, or risk avoidance strategies. Or he can attempt to increase his resources by one means or another in order to realize his communicative intentions. These strategies we can call *resource expansion strategies*. These are clearly 'success oriented' though risk-running strategies.

(p. 17)

The two options set out by Corder are the attempt to either change or modify the intended message, or to change or modify the means of expression. These possibilities exhaust the range of options available to a speaker, and the central feature of his analysis is the need to maintain a balance between the two. As he correctly notes, moreover, this analysis of communication is just as relevant for native-speaker speech as it is for the speech of second-language learners.

A second description of communication relevant for the use of strategies is one proposed by Jakobson (1960). He claims that there are two primitive language-forming acts: *vertical*, involved with selecting, and *horizontal*, involved with combining. These are described by Bruner (1986) in the following way: 'The vertical axis of selection is dominated by the requirement of preserving or modifying meaning by substituting appropriate words or expressions for one another ... The horizontal axis is inherent in the generative power of syntax to combine words and phrases' (p. 22).

The problem of selection is endemic to all speech. Bruner argues that this vertical process lies at the centre of what we consider to be highly literate uses of language. Thus, in ordinary speech we may choose between *boy, immature lad*, and *male*, depending on our purposes, but in poetry our choices may be more widespread, and the result more consequential. Thus, the range of options *depression, black mood*, and *ragged claws scuttling across the floors of silent seas* not only mark the difference between ordinary conversation and poetry, but also between mundane poetry and the exalted heights reached by T. S. Eliot in 'The Lovesong of J. Alfred Prufrock'.

The horizontal process of combination takes as the issue the way in which forms can combine to preserve the selected meanings. No modification of those intentions results from the horizontal process, only the clearer expression of them.

Finally, in the previous chapter it was shown how a two-strategy classification proposed by the Nijmegen group appeared capable of accounting for all the variance in referential communication. These were called the *conceptual* and *code* strategies. The conceptual strategy referred to the manipulation of the concept through a description of its features or a comparison with a similar concept. Features relevant to the identification of the concept were selected and manipulated so that the listener could reconstruct the speaker's intention. The code strategy referred to the selection of some linguistic system to convey this intended concept, without applying any manipulation, decomposition, or comparison to the concept itself.

Basis of Binary Systems

What the three approaches have in common is their basic dichotomy between intention and expression. The process of communicating is the struggle to achieve precision in expression for a set of communicative goals. Put this way, the tension created between intention and expression is a universal feature of communication. How, then, can the communication strategies of second-language learners be conceptualized such that this pervasive feature of all communication is respected, yet the unique qualities of communication by second-language learners are preserved?

The principal criterion for classifying communication strategies must be a processing difference. Communication involves choice, and strategies for making those choices must differ from each other in some psychologically real sense. One clear means of marking a psychologically real difference in choice is through dependence on different forms of processing.

Classifications developed for the purpose of linguistic description need not, of course, conform to this criterion. To this end, the taxonomies based on surface structure differences of utterances provide an inventory of the linguistic possibilities for expressing a given idea. But the argument presented here is that these linguistic possibilities do not constitute strategies in that they do not capture the cognitive choices available to speakers during communication. *Circumlocution* and *paraphrase*, that is, are not different strategies because they do not invoke different processes.

Communication strategies are part of the process of ordinary language use. They reflect the ways in which the processing system extends and adapts itself to the demands of communication. Sometimes traces are left as the system strains to achieve the balance between intention and expression. These are the cases in which noticeable gaps are evident between what one is expected to say, or what would normally say under the circumstances, and what one is able to say. This imbalance is a constant feature of the speech of young children and second-language learners. But sometimes no traces are left, as when parents adjust their speech to accommodate the competence of their young children, teachers adjust their explanations for the sake of their students, and poets adjust their descriptions to achieve grace and depth of meaning.

Analysis and Control in Communication Strategies

The framework consisting of the two processing components permits a mapping of unique strategies on to each of these components. The first strategy is to examine and manipulate the intended concept, capturing Corder's idea of intention. The extent to which one can succeed in this is limited by extent to which the concept is represented as analysed knowledge. The second strategy is to examine and manipulate the chosen form or means of expression, capturing Corder's idea of expression. The extent to which one can succeed in this is limited by the extent to which the speaker has control over the linguistic processes.

The two strategies are operationalized as the enhancement of one of the two processing components. Processing proceeds as usual, as an interaction between the functions of analysis and control, but the reliance on one of the two underlying components of that process is emphasized. Thus an imbalance in processing is created to offset an imbalance in competence.

Analysis-Based Strategy The strategy of exploring the intended meaning takes many forms. It is a frequent feature of native-speaker speech as well as that of second-language learners. Lacking the most direct label for a concept, speakers would normally attempt to provide some distinctive information about that concept. But the success of the strategy, in terms of the utility and appropriateness of the selected information, depends on the extent to which the concept is represented as analysed knowledge.

Conceptual knowledge, or knowledge of the world, is coded as relations. The process of analysis makes these relations explicit by extracting them from contextualized domains of meanings and representing them as relational structures. Symbolic knowledge, then, is explicit knowledge of structure. Knowledge of the world cannot be stored as lexicon because that would make it specific to a particular language. Instead, analysed conceptual structure is independent of the particular language that may have been involved in learning about that domain of knowledge, although the linguistic labels for referring to the structure can of course be represented. Thus, children may learn about categories of fruits and vegetables and their relation to living and nonliving things in French. But when these biological structures become represented as symbolic knowledge, they are equally available to any language that the child then learns. Learning English, then, does not require that the child reanalyse the biological status of known entities. Similarly, analysis of linguistic structure leads to representations of structure that are not tied to the particular language from which they were derived. Accordingly, once children have sorted out concepts such as form class, predication, synonymy, and the like, they can be applied to any particular language. In this way, symbolic representation of knowledge makes that knowledge accessible at a level not possible for implicit unanalysed knowledge. Most importantly, symbolic representation makes explicit structural relations among words, concepts, and entities. It is these relations that are exploited in the analysis-based strategy.

From this point of view, then, analysed knowledge of language includes knowledge of the features and organizing principles of the structure of concepts. Analysed knowledge of concepts includes similar information − what category the concept belongs to, what the distinctive features are, what the function is, and the like. Because of the intimate connection between language and concept, representation of lexicon is structured in the same way as is the representation of these concepts. Thus, the analysis of linguistic knowledge at the level of vocabulary is equivalent to and dependent upon the analysis of conceptual knowledge for those terms. Children must structure both domains as they build conceptual knowledge of the world. Hence, the children in the studies by Snow discussed in chapter 6 and by Dickson discussed in chapter 5 were not always able to identify relevant information for communicating a given intention. But adults in general need only to structure and analyse the linguistic domain as they build a new lexicon to serve the expressive functions of a conceptual structure already constructed through another language.

The analysis-based strategy is an attempt to convey the structure of the intended concept by making explicit the relational defining features. Speakers examine (not necessarily consciously) their symbolic representations of conceptual and linguistic structures in order to select features that will most accurately define the intended meaning. The strategies from the descriptive taxonomies that are included in the analysis-based strategy are circumlocution, paraphrase, transliteration, and word coinage where the attempt is to incorporate distinctive features into the expression, and mime where the attempt is to convey important properties.

Control-Based Strategy   The second strategic option inherent in the processing framework is the manipulation of form of expression through attention to different sources of information. In this strategy, communication is achieved by holding constant the initial intention but altering the means of reference. The predominant means of effecting this manipulation is through switching the language. In processing terms, the strategy is to switch attention away from the linguistic system being used and focus instead on some other symbolic reference system that can achieve the same communicative function.

The primary mechanism of control of processing is selective attention. In the process of planning and participating in speech, many sources of information and possibilities for expression are presented, and the choice of medium is one of those choices. Any decision regarding the channel of expression is a function of control, so any change in that course is a control strategy.

The most common substitute system is another language, but gestures, objects, and other symbols also serve this purpose. At the same time, appealing to others for assistance, or consulting sources such as dictionaries, similarly rely on the control processes for directing attention. Consider the problem of conveying the concept *flute*[1] in the absence of the correct label. One possibility is to point to a flute, should one be so fortuitously available. This strategy could be called something like *ostensive definition*. A second option could be to act out the action of playing a flute. Normally, this would be coded as mime.[2] Alternatively, the speaker may just say the word in another language, such as *fluit* from Dutch. This solution would normally be regarded as something like language switch. But all of these choices are examples of the same strategy if the criterion for classification is not surface form but underlying processing. In each case, a different decision was made about what information should be attended to. All the information is normally available; it is simply not all normally made the focal point of communication. Attention to specific aspects of that information succeeds in conveying the concept. It is also the case that each of the chosen representational systems makes explicit different types of information about the intended concept. The ostensive definition pointed to its shape; the mime pointed to its function; the language switch pointed to its label, albeit in another language. Thus, in a control strategy, one chooses a representational system that is possible to convey and that makes explicit information relevant to the identity of the intended concept.

There are, it seems, predictable occasions on which the control strategy will be used. First, because of its limited dependence on linguistic knowledge, and in particular, on the analysis of that knowledge, the strategy is frequently characteristic of the speech of second-language learners at lower levels of proficiency.

Second, control strategies tend to reduce processing demands by turning attention away from a difficult problem and finding some other means of solution. Hence, situations which compound the processing demands increase the likelihood of using a control strategy. Some evidence for this hypothesis is available from a study in the Nijmegen project (Poulisse, 1989). In a comparison of an object description task, a story-retelling task, and an interview, there was an increasing use of their *linguistic* (code) strategy that corresponded to that order of tasks. These tasks impose increasing burdens on processing. Object description is concerned with a single object, no discourse, no time constraints, no feedback, and no comprehension checks. Story-retelling imposes memory constraints, translation demands (they heard the story in Dutch and had to retell it in English), and requires a coherent discourse structure. Interview is more demanding in that it carries all the discourse demands of story-retelling but requires on-line processing and monitoring as well. So as these processing demands increased, so did the use of a control strategy.

Finally, the control strategy can be expected to be used in situations where there is no conceptual confusion but simply a labelling problem. Here native speakers may make judicious use of the strategy, and sometimes even solve such a problem by appealing to a word in another language, one that perhaps has no connection to the conversation at hand.

Relation to Other Descriptions   Each of the three descriptions of strategic communication considered at the beginning of this section partially reflects the difference between the analysis and control components of language processing. In Corder's definition, manipulation of the intended concept corresponds to the analysis-based strategy and manipulation of the intended form, to the control-base strategy.

Jakobson's two language-forming processes do not divide so perfectly along these lines. The vertical process responsible for selection seems clearly enough to embody analysis of knowledge; the horizontal process responsible for combination corresponds more or less to a restricted interpretation of control of processing. Since communication, especially oral face-to-face interaction, involves more than formal linguistic manipulation, control is also imbued with the responsibility of attending to all relevant forms of expression, both linguistic and nonlinguistic.

The two strategies identified in the Nijmegen project similarly map on to the two underlying components for analysis and control. The conceptual strategy requires analysis of the concept so that the features, images, and classes can be identified and selected. The code strategy relies again on control to switch attention to another system that may solve the problem, or to turn attention to formal features of the code itself.

The distinction posited by Blum and Levenston (1978) between strategies that are process-initiating and strategies that are situation-bound may also reflect an aspect of the distinction between the analysis-based and control-based strategy. Process-initiating strategies result in long-term changes in the representation of the speaker's knowledge of language. This is an analysis function. Situation-bound strategies are attentional procedures for solving a local problem and have no effect on the speaker's representation of the forms or structures of the language. This is a control function.

A cognitive basis for the distinction between analysis and control can be found in the work of Jackendoff (1987). Working within the computational metaphor, he develops a rich description of processing, taking seriously questions of representation and operation to explain cognitive functioning. The model he posits is a detailed explanation of how a cognitive system can function in the domains of language, spatial knowledge, and music. In the model, he describes two functions assigned to attention. The first is called the *selecting function*. Assuming that mental representations contain multiple associations with each other, greater levels of detail than are needed for specific problems, and plurifunctional status with regard to relevant problems, the selecting function is the attentional process that determines what representations get called up in the service of a particular problem and the level of detail that is necessary. The second is called the *directing function*. Having activated a particular representation in working memory, the next attentional function is to focus on the pertinent parts. The selecting function bears some resemblance to analysis of knowledge (but the mapping is not perfect). The point of analysis is to represent knowledge in a symbolic structure of increasing levels of detail. The point of the selecting function is to call up these representations in response to problems. The directing function is closely related to control of processing. Both constitute the process of selective attention to relevant aspects of a representation. At the same time, both involve ignoring irrelevant information that may be misleading. Thus, Jackendoff formalizes the two processes of selecting (cf. analysis) and directing (cf. control) attention in a general account of cognition.

Criteria for Evaluating Strategies

The criticisms of previous approaches to the definition and identification of communication strategies were based on the underlying criteria and assumptions they embodied. In chapter 1, three criteria intrinsic to the definitions were isolated and argued to be overly restrictive. These were the criteria of problematicity, consciousness, and intentionality. In chapter 4, two fallacies inherent in both the definitional and taxonomic approaches were proposed. These were the fallacies of uniqueness and modularity.

Definitional Criteria As we have seen, all communication can be construed as 'problem-solving', as one continually strives to tailor the message to the listener and to achieve the greatest possible precision of expression. While some communicative situations may be described as more problematic than others, it would be impossible to determine a boundary between communication which presents some degree of challenge and communication which is entirely unencumbered by problems. Throughout the range of difficulties, communication proceeds as the interaction of control of processing with representations of language that have achieved specific states of analysis.

Consciousness, too, may be a meaningful description of some extreme endpoint of a dimension. Clearly, different situations exact different levels of monitoring and control over ongoing processing. Similarly, mental representations which are highly explicit, that is, analysed, are more amenable to conscious inspection than are those which are less so. But a categorical boundary between processing which is conscious and that which is not seems not to exist, and so the use of such a boundary as a criterion for describing a phenomenon is inevitably ineffectual.

Finally, intentionality is similarly irrelevant to the operation of the processing framework. Speakers may certainly take charge of processing through the control component, guiding and directing attention to serve specific ends. But such self-direction is not necessary. The processing system works in balance, each skill component stretching to accommodate for a weakness in the other in the service of an overall goal or intention. Speakers rarely choose and honour a specific communication strategy. The simple fact that has beleaguered the analyses of data obtained to investigate the taxonomic classifications is that learners use multiple strategies to convey a single meaning, combining them in ways that are both systematic and creative, shaping those strategies to serve the present purpose. Were strategy selection intentional, we would expect systematic choice – certain kinds of learners in certain kinds of situations would be more likely to choose certain kinds of strategies. The general lack of predictability in choice and the absence of pure examples of single strategies militates against the interpretation that these strategies have been *selected* by learners in some intentional way to solve a perceived problem.

Fallacies of Assumptions The two fallacies are both obviated by this processing conception of communication strategies. The uniqueness fallacy, which was particularly problematic for the definitional approach, led to the assumption that the description of communication strategies used by second-language learners was a distinct phenomenon. In the present approach, these strategies are no different from, and entirely continuous with, the strategies used by any speaker in any form of communication.

The modularity fallacy, in which linguistic products are taken as evidence for psychological processes, is circumvented as linguistic structure has little or no bearing on the interpretation of the strategy. In the present approach, different strategies are determined by different underlying psychological processes and not by different linguistic forms. Thus there are only two distinctive strategies, reducing considerably the explanatory baggage necessary to accommodate them.

The modularity fallacy also led to a description of communication strategies as being a distinct form of language use for second-language learners, discontinuous from other uses of the system. In the present framework, communication strategies are a natural consequence of language proficiency in which two related processing components struggle for a balance to achieve successful communication.

Strategies for Other Uses of Language

The conceptualization of communication strategies as reflecting two components of language processing can also be fruitfully applied to a different set of language strategies. In her work exploring the uses of language for reading, learning, and instructing, Brown and her colleagues (Brown, 1980; Brown, et al., 1983) have identified five strategies for reading. These are as follows:

1 Clarifying the purpose of reading
2 Identifying important aspects of the message
3 Focusing attention on major aspects, not trivia
4 Monitoring comprehension
5 Taking corrective action if failure occurs.

These strategies can be shown to be based on extensions of the same two processing components of analysis and control that underlie other uses of language. The first two strategies, clarifying and identifying, are analysis-based strategies. The reader must have an explicit conception of the goal and meanings of reading, and these must be represented as analysed knowledge. The next two strategies, focusing attention and monitoring, are control-based strategies. The reader must balance and integrate the focus of intention on the multiple dimensions of information while reading. Finally, taking corrective action if failure occurs relies on both analysis and control, the premium component depending upon the sort of action that is taken. Thus, the same two skill components that enable communication similarly motivate the use of language for reading and studying.

Summary of Process Analysis

The definition of communication strategies that follows from this framework is that they are the dynamic interaction of the components of language processing that balance each other in their level of involvement to meet task demands. What is achieved by basing the range of communication strategies on a simple dichotomy between two aspects of language processing? The risk of such a simplification would be in the loss of important variance, that is, the obscuring of relevant differences among some of the events that had been previously recognized as separate strategies. The claim here is, of course, that there is no loss of detail, but a considerable gain in explanatory power.

Different theories are different ways of describing a set of events. To some extent, the difference between theories reflects a difference in the problems identified as the necessary object of explanation. Each type of theory is constructed in the service of a goal. The motivating assumption throughout the present analysis has been that observable events of language behaviour and descriptions of language proficiency must be rooted in the mechanisms of some system that learns, processes, and uses language. Moreover, the stronger claim is that this approach is additionally a general one, encompassing issues from other, more specific purposes. Thus, this processing conception incorporates the observable facts of acquisition and use, and, as shall be argued in the next chapter, the exigencies of language instruction.

8 Learning and Teaching Communication Strategies

There are, it appears, a finite number of strategies that are used by second-language learners when communicating with an inadequate linguistic system. Yet, in spite of the fact that subjects in various research studies used roughly the same strategies and invariably achieved some form of communication, it is also the case that some individuals succeeded more elegantly, more efficiently, or more correctly. The ability to solve problems of this type may be an aspect of a person's strategic or communicative competence. The final issue to be considered is whether or not such competence, or communicative ability, can be taught and developed through formal teaching, perhaps in the same way as we aim to develop a student's syntactic knowledge or command of vocabulary for the target language.

It was shown in chapter 1 that the pedagogical implications of teaching cognitive strategies to children depended on the explanation of those strategies in some functioning model. Similarly, the prognosis for teaching language learners about communication strategies will depend on how those strategies have been conceptualized. Two accounts of communication strategies have been reviewed in this book, and each leads to a different set of consequences for teaching and learning about communication strategies. The two accounts are a taxonomic classification and a process description.

Approaches to Teaching Communication Strategies

Deciding what content would form a reasonable curriculum for the teaching of communication strategies depends on first, what one considers the distinct strategies to be, and second, whether those strategies consist of information, rules, or procedures that can be taught to students. Even if instruction includes a variety of naturalistic activities, the content of strategies and their 'teachability' still need to be determined.

General suggestions for the direction that instruction in communication strategies should take have sometimes been given with the theoretical descriptions. Corder (1983), for example, addressed the problem of conceptualizing strategies by defining their critical features and distinguishing between different varieties or subclasses (see the discussion in chapter 2). He extended that description to its pedagogical implications and stated:

> If one wishes at this stage of the art to consider the pedagogical implications of studying communicative strategies, then clearly it is part of good language teaching to encourage resource expansion strategies and, as we have seen, successful strategies of communication may eventually lead to language learning.
>
> (p. 17)

In this way, he not only set apart a conceptual distinction between types of communication strategies but also invested the greater promise for instruction in one of these. In his terms, the wisdom or necessity of teaching communication strategies is uncontroversial. The nature of that instruction and the content embraced by it, however, is left unspecified.

Kellerman (in press) identifies two approaches to the question of content which he terms the *strong* and *moderate* views. When the strong view is employed, the taxonomic listings are interpreted literally and students are taught paraphrase, word coinage, transfer, and the like. When the approach is that of the moderate view, strategies are presented more generally as possible ways of solving communication problems. Students are made aware of these problem-solving devices and taught to use them in their own communication. Thus, in the strong view, language learners are taught how to solve communication problems, while in the moderate view, they are taught only that communication problems can be solved. The strong view, it will be argued, follows from accepting the taxonomic classifications as explanations of communication strategies; the moderate view follows from placing communication strategies in a processing framework.

The Strong View of Instruction

The strong view of instruction follows from extending the taxonomic classifications to serve as explanations of communicative behaviour. The strategies listed in the taxonomies are considered to be distinct solutions to communication problems. Accordingly, students need to learn the range of solutions and the ways in which they can be effectively applied. Instruction, then, is organized around the taxonomic classifications and students are given the opportunity to learn how to apply these strategies to achieve specific communicative goals (presumably through practice in communicative tasks).

There are two defences offered in support of the strong view of instruction.[1] First, it is claimed[2] that language learners need to learn the strategies and the linguistic means of expressing them so that they will have the resources to solve problems in communication. Students, that is, need to learn both the types of strategic solutions that can be used, circumlocution, approximation, and the linguistic devices for carrying out the descriptions. The curriculum may include such phrases as *It looks like a, You use it for, It's a,* and the like.

Second, it is argued that students need to learn to recognize the occasions when these strategies can be applied. Language learners, that is, do not spontaneously realize the appropriate conditions under which they can implement the communication strategies (irrespective of how the strategies have been learned). Thus, there may be contexts in which it is proper to use a circumlocution, for example, and students need to be taught how to identify these situations. Instruction would include practice of this type.

None of this is problematic. Indeed, any instruction that helps students to master part of the language or to become more comfortable using it is to be commended and not criticized. But what has the student learned about strategies from this approach? Two sources of criticism lead to some doubt about this strong view being the most appropriate approach to instruction. The first is the nature of the taxonomies and their basis in language use; the second is empirical evidence for the success of teaching specific strategies.

The view that the taxonomic classifications correspond to the decisions made by speakers when communicating has been challenged at several points throughout this book. Three points from this argument bear on the problem of directly teaching the strategies as is specified in the strong view.

First, it was argued in chapter 4 that the classification of strategies into the distinctions used by linguistic taxonomies lacks psychological validity. The distinctions, that is, are descriptions of utterances and not descriptions of learners' solutions. Thus, students would be taught the linguistic alternatives for expressing different solutions without being taught how those solutions relate either to the problem or to each other.

Second, selecting which of these strategies to use was shown to depend primarily on context – the features of the object that are critical to the conversation or salient for the concept will be selected and conveyed in whatever means possible. How would students be taught to select the relevant features, especially if they are so dependent on context? Research from children's referential communication (chapter 5) suggests that in any case young children already know how to do this.

Finally, the classification of a strategy to one of the categories was often accidental – *airball* could easily have been *ball with air*, eliminating one of the important (arguably *only*) examples of word coinage in the literature. Accordingly, teaching language learners about the various means for expressing a concept (make it into a word, transfer from your first language, describe its properties) is difficult when those different means themselves cannot be distinguished with certainty.

These areas of indeterminacy in the conceptualization of the communication strategies as taxonomic classifications weakens the use of the taxonomies as a basis of curriculum.

The second source of criticism that disputes the viability of teaching at the level of specific strategies comes from intervention research with cognitive problems. Training studies have frequently been unsuccessful where training was based on specific techniques rather than on general operating solutions. One example is a study by Scardamalia and Paris (1985). Their purpose was to teach high-school students how to write texts that were more coherent. Skilled writers use several strategies for making texts coherent, one being the use of explicit discourse markers such as *although, for example, in contrast, the first point,* and the like. These discourse markers were taught to students as means of structuring and signalling the argument being developed in their essays. An analysis of post-instruction essays written by these students showed that the frequency with which these terms were used increased dramatically, but the essays were no more coherent than they had been before. The students had learned a set of linguistic devices that could be classified on some surface-structure basis, but they had not learned the fundamental problem of selecting, combining, and expressing information. A similar outcome could be expected from training second-language learners in the linguistic devices listed in the communication strategy taxonomies.

A second limitation of training based on specific techniques is raised by Brown et al. (1983). They report numerous examples of subjects trained in specific learning strategies who fail to apply the strategy spontaneously to a new situation. They summarize the failure to transfer as follows:

> These data could be explained if the subjects did not know why rehearsal was helpful or even that it was helpful, that is, if the subjects did not understand the significance of the activities ... In this context, the failure to find transfer of instructed routines could be assumed to result from an incomplete treatment of the initial problems responsible for the strategy deficits.
>
> (p. 133)

Transfer, they argue, requires training in self-regulatory or executive functions.

Minimally, then, instruction must include an explanation to the learner of the way in which the strategy functions to facilitate performance. An analysis of why certain learners failed to employ the usual communication strategies would undoubtedly reveal problems more fundamental than their lack of awareness of these strategies as solutions. An explanation for the deployment of communication strategies, that is, goes beyond the listing of those strategies in a linguistic taxonomy.

None of these procedures are, of course, ruled out by instruction using the strong view. It is possible to teach students about the strategies listed in the taxonomies at the same time as they are being taught more general executive principles for using strategies. The main point is that explicitly teaching students about the different strategies is, in itself, unlikely to improve their ability to communicate.

The Moderate View of Instruction

The moderate view of instruction follows from process descriptions of communication strategies, such as the one outlined in chapter 7. A fundamental difference between the conceptualization of strategies in the taxonomic approach that leads to the strong view of instruction and the conceptualization of strategies in the process approach that leads to the moderate view is where partitioning occurs. In a taxonomic approach, the relevant distinctions are between *strategies*; therefore students need to learn about circumlocution, transfer, etc. In a process approach, the relevant distinction is between *processes*; therefore students need to learn how to analyse and control their linguistic systems. Partly because of this difference, the moderate view is considerably less prescriptive than the strong view in determining instructional procedures. An examination of how the moderate view may be successfully applied to strategy training can be carried out for a related area – teaching effective communication strategies for children to use in their first language.

A considerable body of research has accumulated in which children are studied for their ability to engage in referential communication in their first language (see chapter 5 for a review). Children differ in their ability to use language in this way and a number of training programmes have been effective in improving children's performance. An inventory of successful training procedures used with children is potentially adaptable for use with adult second-language learners.

Two competing hypotheses about why children fail on referential communication tasks have been offered and tested empirically (Kahan and Richards, 1986). The first is that children differ in some relevant cognitive style that endows some children with more effective communication strategies than others (Ammon, 1981). The second is that children suffer information-processing constraints that limit their ability to use language effectively for communication (Shatz, 1978). The results of all these studies indicate that the limiting factor in performance on referential communication tasks is information-processing capacity. Kahan and Richards (1986) showed how older children first recognized the appropriate strategy, even if they could not use it, and finally were able to produce it spontaneously. Individual differences between children regarding their cognitive style or use of contextual information were irrelevant to performance. Similar results were obtained by Brown et al. (1987). They concluded: 'it is clear that children may often have quite sophisticated communicative strategies available to them. Whether or not these strategies emerge may depend on the perceived task requirements, and also on the information-processing demands of the task' (p. 538).

The interpretation that follows from studies such as these is that there is little point in teaching strategies *per se*. The children suffer from an insufficient basis in language processing, and it is processing that must be nurtured. With regard to second-language learners, these speakers do not lack a repertoire of possible solutions such as those listed in the taxonomies, but rather the means to deploy those solutions.

The issue of what to teach as a means of enhancing the strategic communication of second-language learners becomes a matter of identifying the information-processing components of that activity. Brown et al. (1983) point out that instructional research in the past decade has moved decisively towards teaching content-free metacognitive strategies. These are the strategies that aim to enhance the executive information-processing skills that are recruited to solve a range of problems.

A specific example of training metacognitive skills for second-language learners comes from research by O'Malley and his colleagues. They studied the learning strategies used by high-school students of ESL (O'Malley et al., 1985a, b). Their study had both a descriptive and an intervention component. For the former, they elicited an inventory of the strategies that the students were using spontaneously in order to master the language. For the latter, specific training in identifiable strategies was provided formally in the classrooms. The inventory of spontaneous strategies is remarkably consistent with the strategies listed by researchers and used in experimental settings.

The training component involved dividing the students into three groups. The first was a control group, who received no specific training. The second was the metacognitive group. They received training in a metacognitive strategy concerned with executive functioning (e.g. selective attention), and a cognitive strategy concerned with a specific cognitive activity (e.g. note-taking). The third was the cognitive group. They received training in a cognitive strategy and in a socio-affective strategy dealing with co-operation and sharing of information. The three groups were given two post-tests: listening and speaking. Although the authors are enthusiastic about the results, the effects were in fact quite modest. No differences in listening scores were obtained among any of the groups. The speaking task, however, revealed important effects of training. The metacognitive group who had been trained using high-level executive strategies scored higher than the control group. The mean score for the cognitive strategy group is lower, falling between that for the other two groups, and is presumably not significantly different from either.

The findings from the research by O'Malley and his colleagues are consistent with the trend reported by Dickson (1982) in his survey of twenty years of training studies in referential communication. Most of the effective training studies identified relevant subskills and trained them in a general way. Children, for example, were taught to be 'active listeners' and were given a plan for eliciting information. Similarly, they were taught 'comparison skills' which enabled them to systematically compare two entities and then describe the differences. Effective referential communication, according to Dickson, is composed of a large number of these component subskills. The basis of these subskills is not necessarily linguistic, but their role in communication is vital. O'Malley et al. (1985a) make a similar point:

Thus, there may not in fact be any learning strategies that are solely related to languages, but rather a subset of general learning strategies of particular use in developing second language skills. This is not to suggest that language learning itself is not distinctly different from other kinds of learning, only that the strategies which facilitate second language learning may be no different from those used with other learning tasks.

(p. 577)

Following the moderate view, then, language learners can benefit to some extent and under some conditions from instruction in choosing and applying effective strategies. Empirical evidence for this claim comes from children learning to use their first language for reading, learning (Brown et al., 1983), or communicating (Dickson, 1982), and young adults learning to master a second language (O'Malley et al., 1985a, b). There was no direct test of the efficacy of teaching communication strategies to second-language learners. But if the patterns obtained in these related fields apply to the area of communication strategies as well, then similar levels of enhancement can be expected if the limiting conditions identified in the other research are met. Moreover, O'Malley et al. (1985b) point out that the reason these strategies work is not that they introduce new approaches or new strategies to the learners, but rather that they make the learners more aware of strategies already in their repertoire and make them realize that they could work.

Instruction in Language Processing

If the argument developed thus far is correct, then one cannot teach communication strategies directly. Indeed, in the most comprehensive review of language teaching to date, Stern (1983) discusses communicative language teaching at some length, but never implies that the strategies for communication can be taught as part of the curriculum.

What instruction can hope to achieve is to enhance the processing skills that are responsible for the effective use of strategies. These are the subskills of analysis and control. Instruction in communication strategies, then, would consist of training aimed at improving mastery of analysis and control over the target language.

Put this way, strategic competence is the ability to use language effectively for communication through analysis- and control-based strategies. These strategies extend the learner's ability to communicate by entering into a delicate balance in which the two components compensate for each other. The processing components of analysis and control, that is, enter into the process of communicating in response to needs set off by an imbalance in the usual operating mechanisms.

Teaching the strategies, in these terms, means equipping the learner with the resources necessary for the high-level functioning of analysis and control.

What is necessary for analysis of the linguistic system is knowledge. Structural information about the language, including rules of grammar, rules of use, vocabulary, and the like, contributes to the learner's analysis of the system. The greater the analysis, the more likely the learner is to develop reasonable hypotheses about how concepts may be expressed in the target language using the analysis-based communication strategies. What is necessary for control of processing is practice. Experience in speaking, listening, reading, and writing, all contribute to the learner's development of fluent procedures for identifying and accessing relevant knowledge, both linguistic and nonlinguistic, that become especially critical to communication when proficiency in the target language is limited. With the cultivation of these skill components, it is argued, will come the effective use of communication strategies.

In Summary

Three points about the nature of communication strategies have echoed throughout this volume. Each has a bearing on one of the features common to most definitions of the communication strategies identified in chapter 1.

First, the communicative strategies used by second-language learners are consistent with descriptions of language processing where no problem is perceived. Strategic language use, that is, is not fundamentally different from nonstrategic language use. This generalization contradicts the notion that communication strategies can be identified on the basis of problematicity.

Second, language learners solve communication problems with remarkable consistency. Moreover, the solutions are, linguistically at least, similar to those found by children attempting to communicate in their first language. The universal dependence upon a small set of these strategies by children and adults under a variety of circumstances contradicts the notion that communication strategies can be identified on the basis of consciousness.

Third, few conditions alter the selection or effectiveness of particular strategies for communicating. The absence of a relation between choosing a specific strategy and solving a certain kind of problem contradicts the notion that communication strategies can be identified on the basis of intentionality. There is some evidence for differences in strategy selection attributable to the learner's proficiency and the processing demands that specific tasks place on a learner's linguistic competence (see the discussion in chapter 7). Strategic choice is predictable not from superficial features of the communicative task but from the learner's cognitive level of sophistication with two processing components. In this way, learners do not actively choose strategies by contemplating a set of options, as the criterion for intentionality would suggest.

All three of these claims deny special status to communication strategies. Strategies are a normal and fundamental aspect of ordinary language processing. They are rooted in the same processing mechanisms as is nonstrategic language use. They are the adjustments to the ongoing processes responsible for language acquisition and use that allow processing to be maintained. They are the means by which a system can perform beyond its formal limitations and communication can proceed from a limited linguistic system. These claims are attested to by the prevalence and consistency of communication strategies among children speaking their first language, adults speaking their native language under a variety of communicative demands, and both children and adults speaking a second language. The strategies observed to be used and found to be effective for adult second-language learners are derived from, and in some cases identical to, the strategies used by children when mastering their first language. The more language the learner knows, the more possibilities exist for the system to be flexible and to adjust itself to meet the demands of the learner. What one must teach students of a language is not strategy, but language.

Notes

CHAPTER 2   IDENTIFYING COMMUNICATION STRATEGIES

1   The outcome of execution is obviously observable, but their claim is that the mental control over execution is not.

CHAPTER 3   TAXONOMIES OF COMMUNICATION STRATEGIES

1   *Waterpipe* is not used in Britain, where the more traditional 'hookah' is used. Hence in British English this item may not present a communication problem.

CHAPTER 4   EMPIRICAL EVALUATION OF THE TAXONOMIES

1   These are new data not previously reported.
2   Originally, it was simply easier to get girls to participate in the study. Eventually, however, it was decided to restrict the study to girls to avoid pairing girls and boys together in the communication task. Such 'cross-gender' communication is already tension-producing for 9-year-olds!
3   The utterances have been transcribed as accurately as possible from the speech of the subjects. The errors were retained to keep the written form as close to the spoken form as could be determined.
4   This conjecture is based on analysing a subset of the partial utterances and comparing the distribution of strategies observed in the subset to the distribution of strategies that were obtained by using the whole utterances. The two distributions were certainly not identical, but they were close. The main difference was that more noncircumlocution strategies occur when partial utterances are used. This subsample was not formally analysed.
5   Although this strategy is called 'conscious', it is not clear that it is any more or less conscious than any of the other strategies. Hence the label may be misleading.
6   Disputes were resolved by the usual autocratic procedures: the senior investigator (EB) simply examined the alternative codings and made a unilateral decision.

CHAPTER 5 COMMUNICATING IN A FIRST LANGUAGE

1 Notice, though, that these would be classified differently according to Clark's three categories: *cutter* would be a word creation and *you row it* would not even make an appearance.

2 Simplification of speech to children is culturally specific and not found in many other cultures. There is little study, however, of the language acquisition of children in cultures in which such simplification is not part of the speech style addressed to children. None the less, these children do, of course, learn language, so simplification cannot be a necessary condition.

CHAPTER 6 INVESTIGATIONS OF SECOND-LANGUAGE USE

1 There are other strategies that are not wholly included either. Mime, for example, can be either a conceptual strategy or a code strategy depending on the information being conveyed. Word coinage is the only example of this type, however, that appears in the data set reported in chapter 4.

CHAPTER 7 LANGUAGE ACQUISITION AND LANGUAGE PROCESSING

1 This example is from Eric Kellerman (personal communication).

2 Kellerman (personal communication) claims that mime is an example of their conceptual strategy, and that would make it correspond to the analysis-based strategy of the present scheme. The trade-off becomes one of weighing more heavily the switch in attention that has produced the strategy or the conceptual status of it in referring to critical aspects of the object, in this case, its function. Both processes have occurred. Choosing which is decisive in the classification of the strategy becomes a matter of theoretical opinion. Having a strategy that invokes both analysis and control processes is perfectly consistent with the system. There is no reason to expect strategies to rely exclusively on only one of these.

CHAPTER 8 LEARNING AND TEACHING COMMUNICATION STRATEGIES

1 There is little empirical research investigating the pedagogy of communication strategies, so descriptions and evaluations of any procedure are somewhat speculative.

2 Again, there is little literature that explicitly addresses these issues. Most of these arguments I have learned through discussion with language teachers and teacher trainers who have dealt directly with the problem of communication strategies in classrooms.

References

Allport, A. (1988) What concept of consciousness? In A. J. Marcel and E. Bisiach (eds), *Consciousness in Contemporary Science*. Oxford: Oxford University Press.

Ammon, P. (1981) Communication skills and communicative competence: a neo-Piagetian process-structural view. In W. P. Dickson (ed.), *Children's Oral Communication Skills*. New York: Academic Press.

Anderson, J. R. (1982) Acquisition of a cognitive skill. *Psychological Review*, 89, 369–406.

Anglin, J. M. (1977) *Word, Object, and Conceptual Development*. New York: W. W. Norton.

Bates, E. (1976) *Language and Context*. New York: Academic Press.

Bates, E., McNew, L. S., MacWhinney, B., Devescovi, A., and Smith, S. (1982) Functional constraints on sentence processing: a crosslinguistic study. *Cognition*, 11, 245–99.

Beebe, L. M. (1983) Risk-taking and the language learner. In H. W. Seliger and M. H. Long (eds), *Classroom Oriented Research in Second Language Acquisition*. Rowley, Mass.: Newbury House.

Ben Zeev, S. (1977) The influence of bilingualism on cognitive strategies and cognitive development. *Child Development*, 48, 1009–18.

Bereiter, C. and Scardamalia, M. (1982) From conversation to composition: the role of instruction in a development process. In R. Glaser (ed.), *Advances in Instructional Psychology*, vol. 2. Hillsdale, NJ: Lawrence Erlbaum.

Berman, R. A. (1986) A step-by-step model of language learning. In I. Levin (ed.), *Stage and Structure: Reopening the Debate*. Norwood, NJ: Ablex.

Berman, R. A. (1987) A developmental route: learning about the form and use of complex nominals in Hebrew. *Linguistics*, 25, 1057–85.

Bernstein, B. (1961) Social class and linguistic development: a theory of social learning. In A. H. Halsey, J. Floud and C. A. Anderson (eds), *Education, Economy, and Society*. Glencoe, Ill: Free Press.

Bialystok, E. (1978) A theoretical model of second language learning. *Language Learning*, 28, 69–83.

Bialystok, E. (1983) Some factors in the selection and implementation of communication strategies. In C. Faerch and G. Kasper (eds), *Strategies in Interlanguage Communication*. London: Longman.

Bialystok, E. (1988a) Aspects of linguistic awareness in reading comprehension. *Applied Psycholinguistics*, 9, 123–39.

Bialystok, E. (1988b) Levels of bilingualism and levels of linguistic awareness. *Developmental Psychology*, 24, 560–7.

Bialystok, E. and Frohlich, M. (1980) Oral communication strategies for lexical difficulties. *Interlanguage Studies Bulletin*, 5, 3−30.

Bialystok, E. and Kellerman, E. (1987) Communication strategies in the classroom. In B. Das (ed.), *Communication and Learning in the Classroom Community*. Singapore: SEAMEO Regional Language Centre.

Bialystok, E. and Swain, M. (1978) Methodological approaches to research in second language learning. *McGill Journal of Education*, 8, 137−44.

Bierwisch, M. (1980) Semantic structure and illocutionary force. In J. R. Searle, F. Kiefer, and M. Bierwisch (eds), *Speech Act Theory and Pragmatics*. Dordrecht, Netherlands: D. Reidel.

Bierwisch, M. (1981) Basic issues in the development of word meaning. In W. Deutsch (ed.), *The Child's Construction of Language*. London: Academic Press.

Bloom, L. (1970) *Language Development: Form and Function in Emerging Grammars*. Cambridge, Mass.: MIT Press.

Bloom, L. (1973) *One Word at a Time: The Use of Single Word Utterances Before Syntax*. The Hague: Mouton.

Blum, S. and Levenston, E. A. (1978) Universals of lexical simplification. *Language Learning*, 28, 399−416.

Blum-Kulka, S. and Levenston, E. A. (1983) Universals of lexical simplification. In C. Faerch and G. Kasper (eds), *Strategies in Interlanguage Communication*. London: Longman.

Bongaerts, T., Kellerman, E., and Bentlage, A. (1987) Perspective and proficiency in L2 referential communication. *Studies in Second Language Acquisition*, 9, 171−200.

Bongaerts, T. and Poulisse, N. (1989) Communication strategies in L1 and L2: same or different? *Applied Linguistics*, 10, 253−68.

Bowerman, M. (1977) The acquisition of word meanings: an investigation of some current conflicts. In P. N. Johnson-Laird and P.C. Wason (eds), *Thinking: Readings in Cognitive Science*. Cambridge: Cambridge University Press.

Bowerman, M. (1982) Reorganizational processes in lexical and syntactic development. In E. Wanner and L. R. Gleitman (eds), *Language Acquisition: The State of the Art*. Cambridge: Cambridge University Press.

Brown, A. L. (1980) Metacognitive development and reading. In R. J. Spiro, B. C. Bruce, and W. F. Brewer (eds), *Theoretical Issues in Reading Comprehension*. Hillsdale, NJ: Lawrence Erlbaum.

Brown, A. L. (1987) Strategic and knowledge base factors that promote flexible access to knowledge in young children. Paper presented at the Society for Research in Child Development, Baltimore, Md.

Brown, A. L., Bransford, J. D., Ferrara, R. A. and Campione, J. C. (1983) Learning, remembering, and understanding. In J. H. Flavell and E. M. Markman (eds), *Handbook of Child Psychology*, vol. III: *Cognitive Development*. New York: John Wiley.

Brown, A. L. and Reeve, R. A. (1986) Reflections on the growth of reflection in children. *Cognitive Development*, 1, 405−16.

Brown, G. D. A., Sharkey, A. J. C., and Brown, G. (1987) Factors affecting the success of referential communication. *Journal of Psycholinguistic Research*, 16, 535−49.

Brown, H. D. (1976) Discussion of 'Systematicity/variability and stability/instability in interlanguage'. In H. D. Brown (ed.), *Papers in Second Language Acquisition. Language Learning Special Issue*, 135−40.

Brown, R. (1958) How shall a thing be called? *Psychological Review*, 65, 14–21.

Brown, R. and McNeill, D. (1966) The 'tip of the tongue' phenomenon. *Journal of Verbal Learning and Verbal Behaviour*, 5, 325–37.

Bruner, J. (1974/5). From communication to language: a psychological perspective. *Cognition*, 3, 255–87.

Bruner, J. (1975) The ontogenesis of speech acts. *Journal of Child Language*, 2, 1–19.

Bruner, J. (1977) Early social interaction and language acquisition. In H. R. Schaffer (ed.), *Studies in Mother–Infant Interaction*. London: Academic Press.

Bruner, J. (1983) *Child's Talk*. New York: W. W. Norton.

Bruner, J. (1986) *Actual Minds, Possible Worlds*. Cambridge Mass.: Harvard University Press.

Bryant P. E. and Goswami, U. (1987) Phonological awareness and learning to read. In J. R. Beech and A. M. Colley (eds), *Cognitive Approaches to Reading*. New York: John Wiley.

Butterfield, E. C., Wambold, C., and Belmont, J. M. (1973) On the theory and practice of improving short-term memory. *American Journal of Mental Deficiency*, 77, 645–69.

Carroll, J. M. (1980) Naming and describing in social communication. *Language and Speech*, 23, 309–22.

Carroll, J. M. (1981). Creating names for things. *Journal of Psycholinguistic Research*, 10, 441–55.

Case, R. (1985) *Intellectual Development: Birth to Adulthood*. New York: Academic Press.

Clark, E. V. (1973) What's in a word? On the child's acquisition of semantics in his first language. In T. E. Moore (ed.), *Cognitive Development and the Acquisition of Language*. New York: Academic Press.

Clark, E. V. (1983) Meanings and concepts. In J. H. Flavell and E. M. Markman (eds), *Handbook of Child Psychology*, vol. III: *Cognitive Development*. New York: John Wiley.

Clark, E. V. and Berman, R. A. (1987) Types of linguistic knowledge: interpreting and producing compound nouns. *Journal of Child Language*, 14, 547–67.

Clark, H. H., and Clark, E. V. (1977) *Psychology and Language*. New York: Harcourt Brace Jovanovich.

Clark, H. H. and Schaefer, E. F. (1987) Concealing one's meaning from overhearers. *Journal of Learning and Memory*, 26, 209–25.

Clark, H. H and Wilkes-Gibbs, D. (1986) Referring as a collaborative process. *Cognition*, 22, 1–39.

Collins, A. M. and Quillian, M. R. (1969) Retrieval time from semantic memory. *Journal of Verbal Learning and Verbal Behavior*, 8, 240–7.

Corder, S. P. (1977) Simple codes and the source of the second language learner's initial heuristic hypothesis. *Studies in Second Language Acquisition*, 1, 1–10.

Corder, S. P. (1978) Language-learner language. In J. Richards (ed.), *Understanding Second and Foreign Language Learning: Issues and Approaches*. Rowley, Mass.: Newbury House.

Corder, S. P. (1983) Strategies of communication. In C. Faerch and G. Kasper (eds), *Strategies in Interlanguage Communication*. London: Longman.

Dechert, H. W. (1983) How a story is done in a second language. In C. Faerch and G. Kasper (eds), *Strategies in Interlanguage Communication*. London: Longman.

Dickson, W. P. (1982) Two decades of referential communication research: a review and meta-analysis. In C. J. Brainerd and M. Pressley (eds), *Verbal Processes in Children*. New York: Springer.

Dockrell, J. and Campbell, R. (1986) Lexical acquisition strategies in the preschool child. In S. A. Kuczaj and M. D. Barrett (eds), *The Development of Word Meaning.* New York: Springer.

Donaldson, M. (1978) *Children's Minds.* Glasgow: Fontana.

Ehri, L. (1979) Linguistic insight: threshold of reading acquisition. In T. G. Waller and G. E. MacKinnon (eds), *Reading Research: Advances in Theory and Practice.* New York: Academic Press.

Ervin-Tripp, S. and Miller, W. (1977) Early discourse: some questions about questions. In M. Lewis and L. A. Rosenblum (eds), *Interaction, Conversation, and the Development of Language.* New York: John Wiley.

Faerch, C. and Kasper, G. (1983a) Plans and strategies in foreign language communication. In C. Faerch and G. Kasper (eds), *Strategies in Interlanguage Communication.* London: Longman.

Faerch, C. and Kasper, G. (1983b) Communication strategies in interlanguage production. In C. Faerch and G. Kasper (eds), *Strategies in Interlanguage Communication.* London: Longman.

Flavell, J. H. (1977) *Cognitive Development.* Englewood Cliffs, NJ: Prentice-Hall.

Flavell, J. H. and Wellman, H. M. (1977) Metamemory. In R. V. Kail Jr and J. W. Hagen (eds), *Perspectives on the Development of Memory and Cognition.* Hillsdale, NJ: Lawrence Erlbaum.

Fodor, J. (1974) *The Language of Thought.* New York: Thomas Crowell.

Fodor, J. (1983) *The Modularity of Mind.* Cambridge, Mass.: MIT Press.

Fodor, J. and Pylyshyn, Z. W. (1988) Connectionism and cognitive architecture: a critical analysis. In S. Pinker and J. Mehler (eds), *Connections and Symbols.* Cambridge, Mass.: MIT Press.

Forrest-Pressley, D. L. and Gillies, L. A. (1983) Children's flexible use of strategies during reading. In M. Pressley and J. R. Levin (eds), *Cognitive Strategy Research: Educational Applications.* New York: Springer.

Frauenfelder, U. and Porquier, R. (1979) Les voies d'apprentissage en langue étrangère. *Working Papers on Bilingualism,* 17, 37–64.

Freedle, R. and Lewis, M. (1977) Prelinguistic conversations. In M. Lewis and L. A Rosenblum (eds), *Interaction, Conversation, and the Development of Language.* New York: John Wiley.

Galvan, J. and Campbell, R. (1979) An examination of the communication strategies of two children in the Culver City Spanish immersion program. In R. Andersen (ed.), *The Acquisition and Use of Spanish and English as First and Second Languages.* Washington, DC: TESOL.

Garrett, M., Bever, T., and Fodor, J. (1965) The active use of grammar in speech perception. *Perception and Psychophysics,* 1, 30–2.

Garvey, C. (1977) The contingent query: a dependent act in conversation. In M. Lewis and L. A. Rosenblum (eds), *Interaction, Conversation, and the Development of Language.* New York: John Wiley.

Gelman, R. and Baillargeon, R. (1983) A review of some Piagetian concepts. In J. H Flavell and E. M. Markman (eds), *Handbook of Child Psychology,* vol. III: *Cognitive Development.* New York: John Wiley.

Genesee, F. (1983) Bilingual education of majority language children: the immersion experiments in review. *Applied Psycholinguistics,* 4, 1–46.

Gould, S. J. (1981) *The Mismeasure of Man.* New York: W. W. Norton.

Grice, H. P. (1957) Meaning. *Philosophical Review,* 66, 377–88.

Haastrup, K. and Phillipson, R. (1983) Achievement strategies in learner/native speaker interaction. In C. Faerch and G. Kasper (eds), *Strategies in Interlanguage Communication*. London: Longman.

Hakuta, K. (1976) A case study of a Japanese child learning English as a second language. *Language Learning*, 26, 284–97.

Halliday, M. A. K. (1975) *Learning How to Mean*. London: Edward Arnold.

Hess, R. D. and Shipman, V. C. (1965) Early experience and the socialization of cognitive modes in children. *Child Development*, 36, 869–86.

Hosenfeld, C. (1979) Cora's view of learning grammar. *Canadian Modern Language Review*, 35, 602–7.

Huttenlocher, J. (1974) The origins of language comprehension. In R. L. Solso (ed.), *Theories of Cognitive Psychology: The Loyola Symposium*. Potomac, Md: Lawrence Erlbaum.

Inhelder, B. and Piaget, J. (1964) *The Early Growth of Logic*. New York: W.W. Norton.

Isaacs, E. A. and Clark, H. H (1987) References in conversation between experts and novices. *Journal of Experimental Psychology: General*, 116, 26–37.

Jackendoff, R. (1987) *Consciousness and the Computational Mind*. Cambridge, Mass.: MIT Press.

Jakobson, R. (1960) Linguistics and poetics. In T. Sebeok (ed.), *Style and Language*. Cambridge, Mass.: MIT Press.

Kahan, L. D. and Richards, D. D. (1986) The effects of context on referential communication strategies. *Child Development*, 57, 1130–41.

Karmiloff-Smith, A. (1986) From meta-processes to conscious access: evidence from children's metalinguistic and repair data. *Cognition*, 23, 95–147.

Keil, F. (1986) On the structure-dependent nature of stages of cognitive development. In I. Levin (ed.), *Stage and Structure*. Norwood, NJ: Ablex.

Kellerman, E. (1978) Giving learners a break: native language intuition a source of predictions about transferability. *Working Papers on Bilingualism*, 15, 59–89.

Kellerman, E. (1984) The empirical evidence for the influence of the L1 in interlanguage. In A. Davies and C. Criper (eds), *Interlanguage*. Edinburgh: Edinburgh University Press.

Kellerman, E. (in press) Compensatory strategies in a second language: a critique, a revision, and some (non-) implications for the classroom. In E. Kellerman, R. Phillipson, L. Selinker, M. Sharwood Smith, and M. Swain (eds), *Research in Foreign Language Pedagogy*. Clevedon: Multilingual Matters.

Kellerman, E., Ammerlaan, A., Bongaerts, T., and Poulisse, N. (in press) System and hierarchy in L2 compensatory strategies. In R. Scarcella, E. Andersen, and S. Krashen (eds), *Developing Communicative Competence*. New York: Harper and Row.

Kellerman, E., Bongaerts, T., and Poulisse, N. (1987) Strategy and system in L2 referential communication. In R. Ellis (ed.), *The Social Context of Second Language Acquisition*. Englewood Cliffs, NJ: Prentice-Hall.

Kellerman, E. and Sharwood Smith, M. (eds) (1986) *Crosslinguistic Influence in Second Language Acquisition*. Oxford: Pergamon Press.

Kogan, N. (1983) Stylistic variation in childhood and adolescence. In J. H. Flavell and E. M. Markman (eds), *Handbook of Child Psychology*, vol. III: *Cognitive Development*. New York: John Wiley.

Krashen, S. D. (1981) *Second Language Acquisition and Second Language Learning*. Oxford: Pergamon Press.

Krauss, R. M. and Weinheimer, S. (1964) Changes in reference phrases as a function of frequency of usage in social interaction: a preliminary study. *Psychonomic Science*, 1, 113–14.

Krauss, R. M. and Weinheimer, S. (1966) Concurrent feedback, confirmation, and the encoding of referents in verbal communication. *Journal of Personality and Social Psychology*, 4, 343–6.

Krauss, R. M. and Weinheimer, S. (1967) Effect of referent similarity and communication mode on verbal encoding. *Journal of Verbal Learning and Verbal Behavior*, 6, 359–63.

Leopold, W. F. (1949) *Speech Development of a Bilingual Child: A Linguist's Record*. Evanston, Ill.: Northwestern University Press.

Littlewood, W. (1984) *Foreign and Second Language Learning*. Cambridge: Cambridge University Press.

Macnamara, J. (1972) The cognitive basis of language learning in infants. *Psychological Review*, 79, 1–13.

Macnamara, J. (1982) *Names for Things: A Study of Human Learning*. Cambridge, Mass.: MIT Press.

Mandler, J. M. (1984) *Stories, Scripts, and Scenes: Aspects of Schema Theory*. Hillsdale, NJ: Lawrence Erlbaum.

McLaughlin, B. (1978) *Second-language Acquisition in Childhood*. Hillsdale, NJ: Lawrence Erlbaum.

McLaughlin, B. (1987) *Theories of Second-Language Learning*. London: Edward Arnold.

Mitchell-Kernan, C. and Kernan, K. T. (1977) Pragmatics of directive choice among children. In S. Ervin-Tripp and C. Mitchell-Kernan (eds), *Child Discourse*. New York: Academic Press.

Naiman, N., Frohlich, M., Stern, H. H., and Todesco, A. (1978) *The Good Language Learner*. Toronto: Ontario Institute for Studies in Education.

Newport, E. L., Gleitman, H., and Gleitman, L. R. (1977) Mother, I'd rather do it myself: some effects and non-effects of maternal speech style. In C. E. Snow and C. A. Ferguson (eds), *Talking to Children*. Cambridge: Cambridge University Press.

Oltman, P. K., Raskin, E. and Witkin, H. A. (1971) *The Group Embedded Figures Test*. Palo Alto, Cal.: Consulting Psychologists Press.

O'Malley, M. J., Chamot, A. U., Stewner-Mananares, G., Russo, R. P., and Kupper, L. (1985a) Learning strategy applications with students of English as a second language. *TESOL Quarterly*, 19, 557–84.

O'Malley, J. M., Chamot, A. U., Stewner-Mananares, G., Kupper, L. and Russo, R. P. (1985b) Learning strategies used by beginning and intermediate ESL students. *Language Learning*, 35, 21–46.

Paribakht, T. (1982) The relationship between the use of communication strategies and aspects of target language proficiency: a study of Persian ESL students. Unpublished doctoral dissertation, University of Toronto, Toronto.

Paribakht, T. (1985) Strategic competence and language proficiency. *Applied Linguistics*, 6, 132–46.

Piaget, J. (1929) *The Child's Conception of the World*. London: Routledge and Kegan Paul.

Piaget, J. (1965) *The Child's Conception of Number*. London: Routledge and Kegan Paul.

Piaget, J. (1971) *Biology and Knowledge*. Chicago: University of Chicago Press.

Piaget, J. and Inhelder, B. (1956) *The Child's Conception of Space*. New York: W.W. Norton.

Poulisse, N. (1987) Problems and solutions in the classification of communication strategies. *Second Language Research*, 3, 141–53.

Poulisse, N. (1989) On the use of compensatory strategies by Dutch learners of English. Unpublished doctoral dissertation, Nijmegen University.

Pratt, M. W., McLaren, J., and Wickens, G. (1984) Rules as tools. *Developmental Psychology*, 20, 893–902.

Raupach, M. (1983) Analysis and evaluation of communication strategies. In C. Faerch and G. Kasper (eds), *Strategies in Interlanguage Communication*. London: Longman.

Reber, A. S. (1976) Implicit learning of synthetic languages: the role of instructional set. *Journal of Experimental Psychology: Human Learning and Memory*, 2, 88–94.

Reber, A. S. and Lewis, S. (1977) Implicit learning: an analysis of the form and structure of a body of tacit knowledge. *Cognition*, 5, 333–61.

Rescorla, L. A. (1980) Overextension in early language development. *Journal of Child Language*, 7, 321–36.

Rescorla, L. A. (1981) Category development in early language. *Journal of Child Language*, 8, 225–38.

Rescorla, L. A. and Okuda, S. (1987) Modular patterns in second language acquisition. *Applied Psycholinguistics*, 8, 281–308.

Ringbom, H. (1987) *The Role of the First Language in Foreign Language Learning*. Clevedon: Multilingual Matters.

Rosch, E., Mervis, C. B., Gay, W. D., Boyes-Braem, P., and Johnson, D. N. (1976) Basic objects in natural categories. *Cognitive Psychology*, 8, 382–439.

Rubin, J. (1975) What the 'good language learner' can teach us. *TESOL Quarterly*, 9, 41–51.

Scardamalia, M. and Paris, P. (1985) The function of explicit discourse knowledge in the development of test representations and composing strategies. *Cognition and Instruction*, 2, 1–39.

Schacter, D. L. (1987) Implicit memory: history and current status. *Journal of Experimental Psychology: Learning, Memory, and Cognition*, 13, 501–18.

Schegloff, E. A., Jefferson, G. and Sacks, H. (1977) The preference for self-correction in the organization of repair in conversation. *Language*, 53, 361–82.

Schlesinger, I. M. (1971) Production of utterances and language acquisition. In D. I. Slobin (ed.), *The Ontogenesis of Grammar*. New York: Academic Press.

Schneider, W. and Shiffrin, R. M. (1977) Controlled and automatic human information processing. I: Detection, search, and attention. *Psychological Review*, 84, 1–66.

Scribner, S. and Cole, M. (1981) *The Psychology of Literacy*. Cambridge, Mass.: Harvard University Press.

Searle, J. R. (1969) *Speech Acts*. Cambridge: Cambridge University Press.

Searle, J. R. (1980) Minds, brains, and programs. *Behavioral and Brain Sciences*, 3, 417–57.

Seliger, H. W. (1984) Processing universals in second language acquisition. In F. R. Eckman, L. H. Bell, and D. Nelson (eds), *Universals of Second Language Acquisition*. Rowley, Mass.: Newbury House.

Selinker, L. (1972) Interlanguage. *International Review of Applied linguistics*, 10, 219–31.

Selinker, L. and Gass, S. (eds) (1983) *Language Transfer in Language Learning*. Rowley, Mass.: Newbury House.

Shatz, M. (1978) The relation between cognitive processes and the development of communication skills. In C. B. Keasy (ed.), *Nebraska Symposium on Motivation*, vol. 25. Lincoln: University of Nebraska Press.

Shatz, M. (1983) Communication. In J. H. Flavell and E. M. Markman (eds), *Handbook of Child Psychology*, vol. III: *Cognitive Development*. New York: John Wiley.

Siegler, R. S. (1987a) The perils of averaging data over strategies: an example from children's addition. *Journal of Experimental Psychology: General*, 116, 250–64.

Siegler, R. S. (1987b) Some general conclusions about children's strategy choice procedures. Paper presented at the Society for Research in Child Development, Baltimore, Md.

Siegler, R. S. and Shrager, J. (1984) A model of strategy choice. In C. Sophian (ed.), *Origins of Cognitive Skills*. Hillsdale, NJ: Lawrence Erlbaum.

Slobin, D. (1973) Cognitive prerequisites for the development of grammar. In C. Ferguson and D. Slobin (eds), *Studies of Child Language Development*. New York: Holt, Rinehart and Winston.

Smith, E. E., Shoben, E. J., and Rips, L. J. (1974) Structure and process in semantic memory: a featural model for semantic decisions. *Psychological Review*, 81, 214–41.

Snow, C. E. (1977) Mother's speech research: from input to interaction. In C. E. Snow and C. A. Ferguson (eds), *Talking to Children*. Cambridge: Cambridge University Press.

Snow, C. E., Cancino, H., Gonzalez, P., and Shriberg, E. (1989) Second language learners' formal definitions: an oral language correlate of school literacy. In D. Bloome (ed.), *Literacy in Functional Settings*. Norwood, NJ: Ablex.

Snow, C. E., Barnes, W., Chandler, J., Goodman, I., and Hemphill, L. (in press) *Unfulfilled Expectations: Home and School Influences on Literacy*. Cambridge, Mass.: Harvard University Press.

Snow, C. E. and Ferguson, C. A. (eds) (1977) *Talking to Children: Language Input and Acquisition*. Cambridge: Cambridge University Press.

Sonnenschein, S. and Whitehurst, G. J. (1984) Developing referential communication. *Child Development*, 55, 1936–45.

Stern, H. H. (1975) What can we learn from the good language learner? *Canadian Modern Language Review*, 31, 304–18.

Stern, H. H. (1983) *Fundamental Concepts of Language Teaching*. Oxford: Oxford University Press.

Sternberg, R. J. (1980) Sketch of a componential subtheory of human intelligence. *Behavioral and Brain Sciences*, 3, 573–84.

Sternberg, R. J. and Powell, J. S. (1983) The development of intelligence. In J. H. Flavell and E. M. Markman (eds), *Handbook of Child Psychology*, vol. III: *Cognitive Development*. New York: John Wiley.

Stroop, J. R. (1935) Studies of interference in serial verbal reactions. *Journal of Experimental Psychology*, 18, 643–62.

Tager-Flusberg, H. (1986) Constraints on the representation of word meaning: evidence from autistic and mentally retarded children. In S. A. Kuczaj and M. D. Barrett (eds), *The Development of Word Meaning*. New York: Springer.

Tarone, E. (1977) Conscious communication strategies in interlanguage. In H. D. Brown, C. A. Yorio, and R. C. Crymes (eds), *On TESOL '77*. Washington, D. C: TESOL.

Tarone, E. (1979) Interlanguage as a chameleon. *Language Learning*, 29, 181–91.

Tarone, E. (1980) Communication strategies, foreigner talk, and repair in interlanguage. *Language Learning*, 30, 417–31.

Tarone, E. (1981) Some thoughts on the notion of communication strategy. *TESOL Quarterly*, 15, 285–95.

Tarone, E., Cohen, A. and Dumas, G. (1976) A closer look at some interlanguage terminology: a framework for communication strategies. *Working Papers on Bilingualism*, 9, 76–90.

Tulving, E. (1972) Episodic and semantic memory. In E. Tulving and W. Donaldson (eds), *Organization of Memory*. New York: Academic Press.

Varadi, T. (1973) Strategies of target language learner communication: message adjustment. Paper presented at the Sixth Conference of the Romanian–English Linguistics Project in Timisoara.

Varadi, T. (1980) Strategies of target language learner communication: message adjustment. *International Review of Applied Linguistics*, 18, 59–71.

Vihman, M. M. and McLaughlin, B. (1982) Bilingualism and second language acquisition in preschool children. In C. J. Brainerd and M. Pressley (eds), *Verbal Processes in Children*. New York: Springer.

Vygotsky, L. S. (1962) *Thought and Language*. Cambridge, Mass.: MIT Press.

Wagner, J. (1983) Dann du tagen eineeee-weisse Platte – an analysis of interlanguage communication in instructions. In C. Faerch and G. Kasper (eds), *Strategies in Interlanguage Communication*. London: Longman.

Watson, R. (1985) Towards a theory of definition. *Journal of Child Language*, 12, 181–97.

Whitehurst, G. J. and Sonnenschein, S. (1985) The development of communication: a functional analysis. *Annals of Child Development*, 2, 1–48.

Witkin, H. A., Oltman, P. K., Raskin, E., and Karp, S. A. (1971) *A Manual of the Children's Embedded Figures Test*. Palo Alto, Cal.: Consulting Psychologists Press.

Wong Fillmore, L. (1979) Individual differences in second language acquisition. In C. J. Fillmore, D. Kempler, and W. S.-Y. Wong (eds), *Individual Differences in Language Ability and Language Behavior*. New York: Academic Press.

Index

Allport, A., 122
Ammerlaan, A., 81, 110, 111, 112
Ammon, P., 94, 143
analogical descriptions, 102–3
analysis of linguistic knowledge, 118–25
  definition of, 118–19
  development of, 124–5
  instruction, 145–7
  mechanisms for, 122–4
  reading and, 137
  representation, 119–22
  strategy, 132–3
Anderson, J. R., 118
Anglin, J. M., 89
artificial intelligence, 117
attention, 134–5
  directing function, 135
  selecting function, 135
  see also selective attention

Baillargeon, R., 86, 120, 127
Bakker-Renes, 100
Barnes, W., 105
Bates, E., 26, 97, 98
Beebe, L. M., 55
Belmont, J. M., 11
Bentlage, A., 110
Ben Zeev, S., 126
Bereiter, C., 129
Berman, R. A., 90, 124
Bernstein, B., 91, 94
Bever, T., 27
Bialystok, E., 18, 23, 41, 42, 44, 47, 49,
  50, 51, 53, 54, 61, 70, 73, 77, 108,
  112, 122, 128, 150, 151
Bierwisch, M., 85, 97

Bloom, L., 90, 93
Blum, S., 16, 17, 23, 24, 51, 135
Blum-Kulka, S., 41, 50, 81
Bongaerts, T., 81, 110, 111, 112
Bowerman, M., 88, 123
Boyes-Braem, P., 89
Bransford, J. D., 8, 10, 11, 137, 142,
  144, 145
Brown, A. L., 7, 8, 10, 11, 137, 142, 144,
  145
Brown, G. D. A., 143
Brown, G., 143
Brown, H. D., 20
Brown, R., 89, 101
Bruner, J., 87, 88, 99, 130
Bryant, P. E., 124
Buhr, 20
Butterfield, E. C., 11

Campbell, R., 50, 91
Campione, J. C., 8, 10, 11, 137, 142,
  144, 145
Cancino, H., 105, 108
Carroll, J. M., 82, 90
Case, R., 11
Chamot, A. U., 144, 145
Chandler, J., 105
children's definition research, 104–9
  and communication strategies,
    107–9
  differences from adult research, 109
children's strategies
  all-purpose terms, 89–90
  overextension, 88–9, 92
  word creation, 90
chunking, 87

Clark, E. V., 22, 38, 88, 90, 91, 92, 98
Clark, H. H., 22, 38, 53, 74, 98, 101, 102, 103, 112
cognitive development, 9
cognitive strategies, 7–11, 29
Cohen, A., 39
Cole, M., 128
Collins, A. M., 38
consciousness, 4–5, 8, 21, 48, 122, 136, 146
conservation, 127–8
control of linguistic processing
  bilingualism, 128–9
  cognitive style, 127
  definition of, 125–6
  instruction, 145–7
  reading and, 137
  representation, 119–22
  schooling, 128
  selective attention, 125, 128, 133
  strategy, 132–3
conversations
  adults', 99–101
  children's, 96–9
  cognitive basis, 99
  conventions of interactions, 98–9
  linguistic basis, 97–9
Corder, S. P., 3, 26, 30, 31, 32, 33, 35, 43, 81, 99, 129, 130, 131, 132, 134, 139

Dechert, H. W., 50
declarative knowledge, 119
definition research
  see children's definition research
definitions
  classification, 106
  importance of, 105
Devescovi, A., 26, 97
Dickson, W. P., 93, 94, 95, 133, 144, 145
Dockrell, J., 91
Donaldson, M., 86, 128
Dumas, G., 39

Ehri, L., 124
embeddedness, 70
episodic memory, 37
Ervin-Tripp, S., 98
execution phase, 20, 22–3, 49

executive processing, 9, 11, 12, 19, 129, 142

Faerch, C., 3, 5, 17, 20, 21, 22, 23, 24, 31, 32, 33, 34, 35, 43, 44, 47, 51, 53, 70, 71, 73, 74, 82, 110
fallacy
  modularity fallacy, 80, 82, 104, 137
  uniqueness fallacy, 80, 81, 104, 136
Ferguson, C. A., 84, 99
Ferrara, R. A., 8, 10, 11, 137, 142, 144, 145
field dependence/independence, 127–8
first language research
  adult, 91–2, 95, 100, 101
  children, 87–90, 91–3, 95, 100–1
Flavell, J. H., 7, 95
Fodor, J., 27, 117, 118
foreignization, 42, 44, 87
form, 32–5, 118, 122, 128, 129, 130, 131
Forrest-Pressley, D. L., 7
Frauenfelder, U., 18, 23
Freedle, R., 98
Frohlich, M., 27, 41, 42, 50, 51, 53, 70, 73, 108

Galvan, J., 50
Garrett, M., 27
Garvey, C., 98
Gass, S., 87
Gay, W. D., 89
Gelman, R., 86, 120, 127
Genesee, F., 59
Gillies, L. A., 7
Gleitman, H., 100
Gleitman, L. R., 100
Gonzalez, P., 105, 108
Goodman, I., 105
Goswami, U., 124
Gould, S. J., 55
Grice, H. P., 96

Haastrup, K., 50, 51, 62
Hakuta, K., 87
Halliday, M. A. K., 97
Hemphill, L., 105
Hess, R. D., 91
Hoefnagel-Hohle, 100

Hosenfeld, C., 27
Huttenlocher, J., 89

individual differences, 29, 143
Inhelder, B., 89, 94, 120, 126
instruction, 11, 95−6, 139−47
  moderate view, 140, 143−5
  strong view, 140−2
intelligence, 5
intentionality, 5, 136, 146
interlanguage, 16, 17, 18, 25, 51
Isaacs, E. A., 103

Jackendoff, R., 118, 135
Jakobson, R., 130, 134
Jefferson, G., 101
Johnson, D. N., 89

Kahan, L. D., 95, 143
Karmiloff-Smith, A., 122, 123, 124
Karp, S. A., 128
Kasper, G., 3, 5, 17, 20, 21, 22, 23, 24,
  31, 32, 33, 34, 35, 43, 44, 47, 51,
  53, 70, 71, 73, 74, 82, 110
Keil, F., 85
Kellerman, E., 52, 73, 81, 87, 110, 111,
  112, 113, 115, 140
Kernan, K. T., 98
Klaus, 20
Kogan, N., 127
Krashen, S. D., 19
Krauss, R. M., 53, 101, 102
Kupper, L., 144, 145

L1, 20, 32, 49, 52−3, 81, 86
L2, 25, 48, 49, 52−3, 81, 86, 105−15
language acquisition, 116−38
language processing, 2, 82, 109, 112,
  116−38
learning strategies, 14, 17, 26, 27−8, 35,
  142, 144, 145
Leopold, W. F., 88
Levenston, E. A., 16, 17, 23, 24, 41, 50,
  51, 81, 135
Lewis, M., 98
literal descriptions, 102−3
Littlewood, W., 75

McLaren, J., 96

McLaughlin, B., 19, 87, 128
Macnamara, J., 86
McNeill, D., 101
McNew, L. S., 26, 97
MacWhinney, B., 26, 97
Mandler, J. M., 37
meaning, 32−5, 118, 125, 126, 128, 129,
  130, 132
  conceptual, 85
  semantic, 85
mental representations, 117, 118, 120,
  123
  types, 123−4
metacognition, 9, 108, 144
metalinguistic, 105, 116, 122, 124, 125,
  126, 128
Mervis, C. B., 89
Miller, W., 98
Mitchell-Kernan, C., 98

Naiman, N., 27
Newport, E. L., 100
Nijmegen project, 110−15, 130, 134,
  135

Okuda, S., 87
Oltman, P. K., 127, 128
O'Malley, J. M., 144, 145
overextension, 88−9, 92

Paribakht, T., 44, 45, 46, 50, 54, 73
Paris, P., 142
Phillipson, R., 50, 51, 62
Piaget, J., 86, 89, 94, 120, 124, 126, 127
planning phase, 20, 22, 49
Porquier, R., 19, 23
Poulisse, N., 81, 110, 111, 112, 134, 135
Powell, J. S., 9
Pratt, M. W., 96
prelinguistic capacities, 98
problematicity, 3−4, 21, 24, 136, 146
problem-solving, 8−9
procedural knowledge, 119
process-analysis
  see Nijmegen project
process-oriented approach, 109
proficiency level, 14, 48−50, 94, 108,
  112, 113
psychological plausibility, 22, 112

Pylyshyn, Z. W., 117

Quillian, M. R., 38

Raskin, E., 127, 128
Raupach, M., 50
reading strategies, 137
Reber, A. S., 120
Reeve, R. A., 8
reliability, 58, 61, 76–80, 115
Rescorla, L. A., 87, 88, 89
research
    see adult strategy research; children's
    definition research; first-language
    research; Nijmegen project;
    second-language research
    linguistic processing, 120
    referential strategies, 110
Richards, D. D., 95, 143
Ringbom, H., 52
Rips, L. J., 38, 88
Rosch, E., 89
Rubin, J., 27
Russo, R. P., 144, 145

Sacks, H., 101
Scardamalia, M., 129, 142
Schacter, D. L., 120
Schaefer, E. F., 103
Schegloff, E. A., 101
Schlesinger, I. M., 93
Schneider, W., 118, 125
schooling, 128
Scribner, S., 128
Searle, J. R., 96, 117
second-language research
    adult, 77–8, 78–80
    children, 58–83
self-reflection, 124
Seliger, H. W., 17, 23
Selinker, L., 6, 11, 25, 26, 87
Sharkey, A. J. C., 143
Sharwood Smith, M., 52, 87
Shatz, M., 94, 97, 99, 143
Shiffrin, R. M., 118
Shipman, V. C., 91
Shoben, E. J., 38, 88
Shrager, J., 9
Shriberg, E., 105, 108

Siegler, R. S., 7, 8, 9
simplification, 16, 18
    of speech addressed to children,
    99–101
Slobin, D., 27
Smith, E. E., 38, 88
Smith, S., 26, 97
Snow, C. E., 84, 99, 100, 105, 106, 107,
    108, 112, 133
social strategies, 28–9
Sonnenschein, S., 93, 96
Stern, H. H., 3, 6, 27, 28, 145
Sternberg, R. J., 9, 19
Stewner-Mananares, G., 144, 145
strategic competence, 96, 145
strategy, 15
    constraints, 16
    for conversations, 100–3
    for definitions, 107–9
    linguistic processing components, 116
    selection, 48–56
    taxonomy, *see* taxonomy
    types, *see* strategy types
    uses for, 116
strategy types
    achievement, 31–2, 43, 47, 71
    compensatory, 44, 50
    message adjustment, 30, 42, 61,
        70–1, 130
    production, 26
    reduction, 31–3, 42, 43
    referential, 110
    replacement, 32–3, 42
    resource expansion strategy, 30, 130
    retrieval strategy, 44
    social strategies, 28–9
Stroop, J. R., 126
structure, 37
    categorical taxonomic structure, 37
    schematic structure, 37
Swain, M., 61
symbol system, 98, 119, 121–2, 127,
    128, 132, 133

Tager-Flusberg, H., 92
Tarone, E., 3, 26, 27, 39, 40, 41, 42, 44,
    47, 48, 52, 53, 55, 57, 61, 62, 70,
    71, 72, 74, 107, 111, 113
task differences, 50–2

taxonomies
  evaluation, 58–83, 112
  weaknesses, 110
taxonomies, types
  appeal for assistance, 41, 44, 55, 62,
    68–9, 74, 77, 79, 87
  avoidance, 40, 44, 55, 61, 62–3,
    70–1, 77, 79
  code, 114–15, 130, 134
  conceptual, 110–15, 130
  conscious transfer, 41, 44, 52,
    66–8, 74, 77, 79, 114, 140
  L1-based, 42, 49, 51, 52
  L2-based, 42, 47, 49, 52, 55
  mime, 42, 44, 45, 50, 62, 133, 134,
    149
  paralinguistic, 42
  paraphrase, 40, 44, 47, 48, 51, 62,
    63–7, 72–4, 77, 107, 109, 131,
    133, 140
  see also Bialystok; Paribahkt; Tarone;
    Varadi
tests
  Children's Embedded Figures Test,
    128

Class inclusion task, 126–7
communication task, 59–60
Conservation of Liquid Task, 127
Embedded Figures Test, 126–7
Stroop Task, 126
Sun/Moon Problem, 126, 128
Todesco, A., 27
Tulving, E., 37

validity, 55, 56, 58, 61, 76–80, 113–15
Varadi, T., 32, 33, 34, 35, 41, 42, 50, 53,
  73
Vihman, M. M., 128
Vygotsky, L. S., 120

Wagner, J., 50
Wambold, C., 11
Watson, R., 108
Weinheimer, S., 53, 101, 102
Wellman, H. M., 7
Whitehurst, G. J., 93, 96
Wickens, G., 96
Wilkes-Gibbs, D., 53, 75, 101, 102, 112
Witkin, H. A., 127, 128
Wong Fillmore, L., 28, 29, 87